A Novel Machine Learning Method for Preference Identification

A Chess Case Study

by

Azlan Iqbal
College of Computing and Informatics
Universiti Tenaga Nasional
Malaysia

*For Noryah and Madelaide (rockstars),
and Ashley… all grown up.*

ISBN 979-8570636583

Copyright © 2020 by Azlan Iqbal
Cover art licensed under Creative Commons (CC0)

Independently published.

This work and all its contents are subject to copyright. All rights are reserved by the author as per agreement with the publisher, whether the whole or part of the material is concerned, specifically the rights of translation, reprinting, reuse of illustrations, recitation, broadcasting, reproduction on microfilm or in any other physical way, and transmission or information storage and retrieval, electronic adaptation, computer software, or by similar or dissimilar methodology now known or hereafter developed. Neither the publisher nor the author give a warranty, expressed or implied, with respect to the material contained herein or for any errors or omissions that may have been made. The contents of this book, unless otherwise stated, reflect only the opinions and thoughts of the author.

Contents

Preface 4

Introduction 6

Chapter 1: Traditional Machine Learning 8

Chapter 2: Changes Between Objects 15

Chapter 3: Statistical Testing 21

Chapter 4: Ranking and the General Algorithm .. 26

Chapter 5: Experimental Results 30

Chapter 6: Conclusions 38

References 43

Appendix A: Programming Code Examples 47

Appendix B: Database Entries 57

Appendix C: Experimental Samples 86

PREFACE

Academic publishing these days can be a complicated affair. There are so many journals and publishers to choose from; each of them having their own individual formats and standards. Never mind conferences, of which there are even more. Among all these, there is the 'predatory' kind and also different indexes which add even further variation in terms of their perceived 'prestige'. I had a choice to publish this work in a journal but I would likely have had to break it into smaller parts and even condense sections I think would be important to reproduce the results experimentally. Fortunately, we live in a time where there are alternatives that also reserve a more reasonable share of the proceeds for the author.

Machine learning (ML) is all the rage now in artificial intelligence (AI). Many even believe it will lead to artificial general intelligence (AGI), and soon. For years, I had avoided jumping on the ML bandwagon until I was faced with a problem in my own field or area of expertise that required it. Unfortunately, I could not find any existing implementation of ML that would work as well as I needed, if at all… so I invented my own; and it has nothing to do with an artificial neural network (ANN). The novel method I propose allows a computer to learn the taste or preferences of a user based on existing 'liked' and 'disliked' selections. The present case study has to do with chess, of course. A domain of AI research I've been working in for about 15 years. While my previous works related to computational aesthetics and then computational creativity, human preference identification actually requires a kind of 'learning' that those previous endeavors did not.

As it stands now, choosing chess problems that one likes from a collection of new compositions is a tedious process. One has to go through all of them and decide which should be retained and which should not. Imagine doing this over and over for hundreds or even thousands of say, computer-generated compositions (a result of earlier research work). There has to be a better way, as the saying goes. This book addresses that very issue in as much detail as I could provide. It is indeed a novel method and I hope it is presented in a way sufficient to be reproduced by anyone or any group of people with the necessary resources and skill sets.

INTRODUCTION

Human preference or taste within any domain is usually a difficult thing to identify or predict with high probability. Especially so when relying on single-user data. In the domain of chess problem composition, the same is true. Traditional machine learning approaches tend to focus on the ability of computers to process massive amounts of data and continuously adjust 'weights' within an artificial neural network (ANN) to better distinguish between say, two groups of objects. Contrasted with chess compositions, there is no clear distinction between what constitutes one and what does not; even less so between a good one and a poor one.

I propose in this book a computational method that is able to learn from existing databases of 'liked' and 'disliked' compositions such that a new and unseen collection can be sorted with increased probability of matching a solver's preferences. The method uses a simple 'change factor' relating to the Forsyth-Edwards Notation (FEN) of each composition's starting position, coupled with repeated statistical analysis of sample pairs from both databases. Tested using my own collections of computer-generated chess problems, the experimental results showed that the method was able to sort a new and unseen collection of compositions such that, on average, 75% of the preferred compositions were in the top half of the collection.

This saves significant time and energy on the part of solvers as they are likely to find more of what they like sooner. The method may even be applicable to other domains such as image processing because it does not rely on any chess-specific rules but rather just a sufficient and quantifiable 'change' in representation from one object to the next.

Chapter 1

Traditional Machine Learning

Machine learning, a term popularized by Arthur Lee Samuel (Samuel, 1959), essentially encompasses computational approaches that help us find meaningful patterns in data; especially without the need to explicitly program the computer to do so. It is generally preferable where traditional rule-based programming does not work as well or at all. Perhaps one of the most dramatic contemporary examples of machine learning progress was the 2016 five-game match between Lee Sedol, perhaps the top go player at the time, and AlphaGo, a computer program designed by Google's 'DeepMind' company (Metz, 2016).

AlphaGo defeated Lee Sedol four games to one; something some experts believed would not happen for another decade or so (Associated Press, 2016; Yan, 2016). Soon after that, their 'AlphaZero' program was generalized enough to be able to master the games of chess, shogi and go (Silver et. al, 2018). In chess, the then world champion, Garry Kasparov, was defeated about two decades earlier in a 1997 match by IBM's 'Deep Blue' computer

(Hsu, 2002). It did not use machine learning like 'AlphaZero' but a brute-force, heuristics-based approach. Since then, chess programs have served more as tools for humans, even master players, to train with rather than compete against (Dhou, 2008; Khadilkar, 2019). A chess app downloaded to a smartphone today is stronger than most grandmasters, and if running on a typical desktop or even notebook computer could likely defeat even the world champion (Newborn, 2011). Unfortunately, this has led some master players to cheat (Friedel, 2017; Chiu, 2019).

The subdomain of chess composition, however, remains relatively immune to AI or machine learning advances. I am not referring to the solving of such problems (existing chess engines do that quite well, if not perfectly, already) but rather the assessment of human preference with regard to aesthetics, interestingness and qualities of that nature. Aspects of chess compositions that are difficult, if not impossible, to quantify but that appeal to people on an individual basis regardless of domain knowledge and experience. In short, is there a way for a computer to learn from a collection of one's personal liked and disliked compositions such that new compositions can be at least sorted in terms of the probability that they will also be liked by the solver?

In general, there are four main categories of machine learning and two main approaches used in recommender systems that I would like to briefly explain here. In this book, the terms chess problem, chess puzzle and chess composition are used interchangeably; 'user' and 'solver' refer to the subject or person in question. The existing categorizations of machine learning, i.e. supervised, unsupervised, transfer and reinforcement were deemed unsuitable for preference identification in chess compositions.

Supervised learning relies on proper labeling of many examples. For instance, in distinguishing between photos of cats and dogs. Chess compositions cannot be reliably labeled in this way. While they can be easily categorized as valid or invalid – a composition is valid if its stipulation (e.g. 'White to play and mate in 3 moves') is found to be true based on say, exhaustive chess software engine analysis – that is just the tip of the iceberg. A particular chess problem may contain one or more chess themes (e.g. pin, fork, skewer) and abide by one or more composition conventions (e.g. no 'check' in the first move, no duals); it could also be paradoxical which means it goes against what is typically taught to chess players (Howard, 1967; Levitt and Friedgood, 2008). Not to mention possessing other qualities such as economical use of pieces and being challenging but not too complex (Margulies, 1977). So, it is not 'one thing' as opposed to 'another thing' such as a cat versus a dog.

Unsupervised learning attempts to find patterns in data without labels and is typically used in anomaly detection. For instance, likely fraudulent credit card transactions (Rai and Dwivedi, 2020).

Anomalies or paradoxical moves in chess problems (and even regular games), on the other hand, are typically sought after, e.g. an unexpected queen or major piece sacrifice (Shenk, 2006). Compared to the original position, a single piece moved to a neighboring square may not look very different or 'anomalous' to an unsupervised learning system but it could change everything about a chess problem or completely invalidate the solution.

Reinforcement learning uses 'rewards' and 'penalties' in order for the system to learn the rules or 'policies' which can be effective in learning to play chess (like with 'AlphaZero') but not really to evaluate what makes a good chess problem or puzzle, especially from the viewpoint of a particular person. This is because the rules of playing and what constitutes a win in a game are usually quite clear whereas what qualifies in terms of personal taste is not. For example, a solver could specify any number of conventions that a chess problem must satisfy yet still encounter many that are not appealing, and furthermore actually miss many that do not satisfy all those conventions yet would have been appealing for other reasons that may not even be explicable by the solver.

Transfer learning relies on using the rules from another system and applying it to your own (Zhuang et al., 2020). In practice, this may involve using the existing and already-trained lower layers of a neural network in some form of say, image detection and simply adding another higher (prediction) layer which helps describe a higher-level image. The new system 'reuses' the lower layers already trained. For chess problems, this would mean depending on an existing simpler and related system that can be applied. Some people might say that 'chess puzzles' are not as sophisticated as 'chess problems' or that the conventions are not as many, even though their definitions imply they are generally interchangeable or at least overlap significantly (Iqbal, 2019). So, if we had an existing set of neural network layers describing chess puzzles, we could simply transfer them to a more sophisticated chess problem network with an additional layer.

Unfortunately, there is no known trained system for chess puzzles to transfer learning from in this case. Furthermore, distinguishing between chess problems and chess puzzles would be difficult, if not impossible, since many 'simpler' or less sophisticated chess problems would closely resemble chess puzzles. A chess puzzle composer may condone or accept having a 'check' in the first or key move, for instance, yet there are also renowned chess problems where the key move starts with a 'check' (Friedel, 2018). This is because exceptions are not uncommon in problem composition, especially if there are compensating factors. At this point, we have not even factored in personal taste or preference yet. Therefore, even transfer learning is unsuitable here.

Recommender or recommendation systems more directly address the aspect of user preference or taste in a variety of domains

(Deldjoo et al., 2020). Two main difficulties arise. The first is that new objects to be evaluated are unseen and unpredictable (i.e. they arise in the future) and the second is that a person's taste or preferences can, and probably will, change with time. One approach is to rely on content filtering or asking users what they like and dislike. For instance, with regard to films, a user may indicate that they like drama and action movies but dislike comedies and musicals. Therefore, a new film which has been classified as largely a mix of action, some drama and a little comedy may be recommended to this user. A new film which is mostly a musical comedy with some action, on the other hand, will not be recommended.

Gathering all this feature data can be cumbersome. It is also problematic because the system only improves (to a point) given more and more features including further details about each user and their preferences, e.g. user nationality, level of education, favorite actors, preferred movie length. This can be burdensome to the user and they are not always particularly good or accurate at describing their preferences either. Often, a user does not know if they will like something until they actually experience it and even then, they are not always able to explain why in a way that would make sense to someone collecting or processing the data.

Another approach is to filter 'collaboratively', i.e. to rely on unknown or 'latent features' that arise from the data (Khenissi et al., 2020). This may refer to the data about users and what they actually watch (and for how long etc.). In practice, because many other 'similar users' also watched another movie, you might find the system recommending it to you as well. The system is able to learn from the patterns found in the data because the data are not random. It is essentially a more precise, effective and dynamic approach to the problem.

The main issue with existing recommendation approaches like these with regard to chess compositions is that there is no known service where a sufficiently large user base experiences them in the way they experience say, music or movies. Even if there is (e.g. an online chess community featuring chess puzzles that can be rated), it is not a localized and personalized learning system that each user can run on their own preference data. Data that are not intermingled or 'contaminated', to an extent, with the preferences of other 'similar people'.

Chapter 2

Changes Between Objects

The initial position of a chess problem (the 'object', in this case) is typically recorded using the standard Forsyth-Edwards Notation (FEN). Figure 1 shows two example positions with their corresponding FENs.

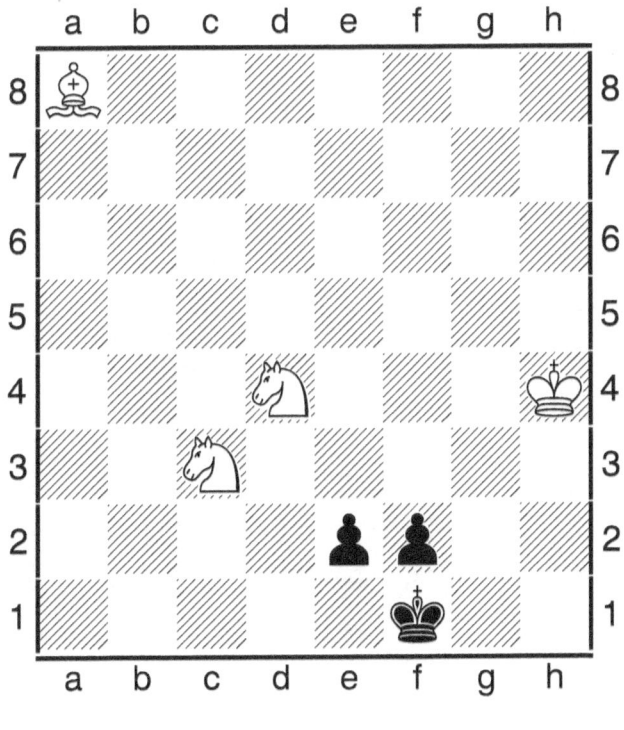

(a) B7/8/8/8/3N3K/2N5/4pp2/5k2 w - - 0 1

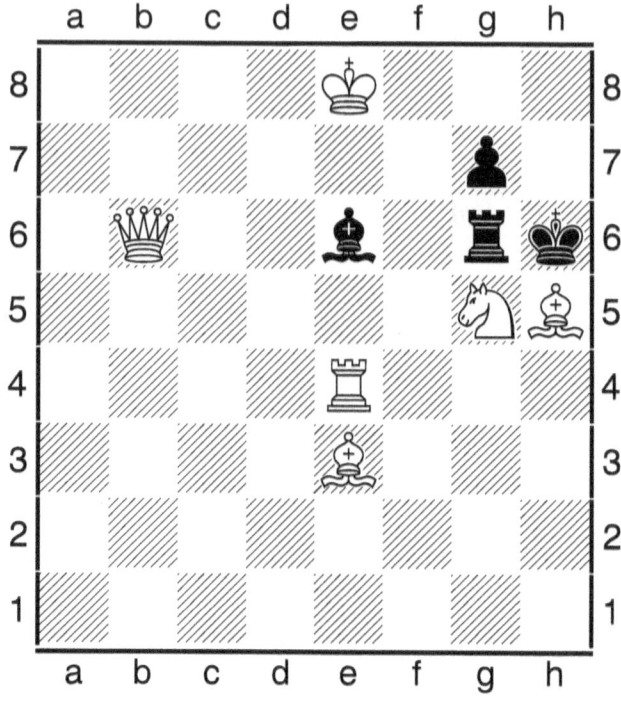

(b) 4K3/6p1/1Q2b1rk/6NB/4R3/4B3/8/8 w - - 0 1

Figure 1: Example chess positions with their FENs.

Each row, starting from the upper left corner is separated by a slash ('/'). Within each row, uppercase letters are used for the white pieces and lowercase letters for the black pieces, e.g. 'K', 'q', 'R', 'b', 'N', 'p'. Empty squares are represented using a digit, such as '1' for a single empty square between two pieces or '3' for a stretch of three empty squares. This is followed by a space and either a 'w' or 'b' to indicate the side to move. The remaining characters have to do with castling permissions, possible 'en passant' capturing, and the number of half-moves (plies) and full moves played. More information about this format can be found in (Wikipedia, 2020). Everything starting with the side to move is irrelevant for our present purposes.

In order to detect changes between FENs, they need to be converted, up to the point of the bottom row information, into a form that is more consistent in length. This is achieved by simply converting all the digits that represent empty squares into '1s' and removing the slashes as well because they cannot change from one position to the next. So, the FEN for Figure 1(a), for instance, would now look like this (but without even the blank spaces every eight characters which have been added here for legibility): 'B1111111 11111111 11111111 11111111 111N111K 11N11111 1111pp11 11111k11'. The same process applied to the FEN for Figure 2(b) would ensure a string of the same length where each character can be compared against the one in Figure 1(b) or any other FEN consistently.

This form sufficiently represents the 'look' of the position. The change from one FEN to the next is based on two simple rules. The first is that if a blank character, i.e. a '1' changes to any piece (e.g. 'K', 'r') or vice versa, then the 'change factor' (CF) as a percentage value is 100, i.e. a total change. The second rule is that if the change is from one piece to another piece (e.g. 'K' to 'Q'), the CF is 50 or a partial change. A blank square to a blank square or a piece to the same piece does not count. These values are accumulated for the entire string and then summed as the 'change value' (CV) between the two FENs. It is noteworthy here that this technique of detecting changes does not rely on any chess-specific rules, which was my intention. It should make the process more generic and widely applicable. Table 1 shows an example of the change value from FEN 1 to FEN 2.

FEN 1	B1111111111111111111111111111111111N111K11N1 11111111pp1111111k11
FEN 2	1111K111111111p11Q11b1rk111111NB1111R1111111 B111111111111111111
CV	[(17/64) x 100] + [(0/64) x 50] = 26.5625

Table 1: Calculated 'change value' (CV) from one FEN to the next.

The first and second FENs have been 'expanded' to their 64-character forms. Each character is compared with its counterpart. There are 17 changes out of 64 that represent a total or 100% change and none which represent a partial change. This works out to 26.5625 or 26.562, if rounded to three decimal places. (Incidentally, '5' in this case being the last available digit in the series means the '2' just before it stays the same and is not incremented to '3' since we do not know if the '5', which is precisely in the middle of '0' and '10' tends upward.)

Using a smaller segment as another example, '1K1Q1' changing to '1K1R1' or '1K1n1' would have a CV of (1/5) x 50 = 10. Another notable quality of this technique is that the FENs can even be reversed and the CV would be the same, i.e. it works in both directions.

Between two positions or FENs, the CV as just explained is fairly easy to calculate. However, given a collection or database of chess compositions, it is necessary for the computer to be able to learn the changes across many positions, perhaps even with newer ones being added from time to time. Using a theoretical example of a sample of seven FENs, the CVs might appear as shown in Table 2.

FEN	CV
1	0
2	26.562
3	27.344
4	25.000
5	17.969
6	11.719
7	14.062

Table 2: The 'change values' in a sample of positions.

The CV from the first FEN to the second is 26.562, the CV from the second to the third is 27.344 and so forth. Since a CV can only be calculated when a FEN is compared to a prior one, the first FEN always has an associated default CV of '0' (as if comparing to nothing or itself). The ordering of these positions, in a sample, is also relevant now. If a different FEN which might otherwise have appeared much later got inserted somewhere in the middle of this sample replacing an existing one, then the CVs for this sample would no longer be the same. This is important because the method proposed uses many (statistical) t-tests between many such samples. While the number of decimal places that should be used for the CVs is not prescriptive, even higher precision than what is seen here may be preferable in some cases.

Chapter 3

Statistical Testing

In order to learn what a particular person's preferences are with regard to chess problems, it is necessary to have a collection of problems that person had seen and selected, i.e. the 'liked' database (LD) to contrast against the problems that person had seen and rejected, i.e. the 'disliked' database (DD). A sample from either database would typically be larger but look like the one shown in Table 2, i.e. FENs with a 'change value' (CV) beside each one. A t-test can then be used to determine if the mean CV is different between the two samples (one from each database) to a statistically significant degree. In the present case, the two-tailed, two-sample t-test assuming unequal variances (TTUV) at the 5% level was deemed suitable. Ideally, the same sample size should be used for both databases.

After some testing, I determined that a variable but incremental sample size of between a minimum of 30 and a maximum of 60 (chosen randomly), repeated for three cycles, worked best, i.e. provided the most consistent results. More specifically, many t-tests are actually performed and this depends on the sizes of the

LD and DD. For example, the LD might have a total of 200 compositions whereas the DD might have 425 compositions. In the first cycle, let us assume the random sample size is say, 32. This means the first 32 CVs of the LD are compared against the first 32 CVs of the DD using the TTUV. Figure 2 shows what these samples could look like. The CVs in it are shown for illustrative purposes only and were not derived from actual FENs. The three dots represent the missing intermediate FENs and CVs.

FEN	CV
1	0
2	16.562
3	26.344
4	23.000
5	17.969
...	...
32	15.062

'Liked' Sample

FEN	CV
1	0
2	27.562
3	17.344
4	26.000
5	19.969
...	...
32	17.162

'Disliked' Sample

Figure 2: Example of samples from two databases.

The TTUV result of the 32 CVs from the LD sample compared against the 32 CVs from the DD sample is recorded as being significant or insignificant. This is the first test (T1). The same t-test is then performed but this time a new FEN under consideration is inserted into the last slot, i.e. 32 of the 'liked' sample, replacing whatever FEN was there and creating a new CV using the 31st FEN and itself. This is intended to aid in determining if the new

FEN 'belongs' in the LD. The significance of the TTUV result returned this second time (T2) is then recorded.

A change from insignificant (in T1) to significant (in T2) counts as a 'positive' (POS) whereas the opposite counts as a 'negative' (NEG). The process is then repeated but against the next sample 'chunk' of the DD. This means the first 32 CVs from the LD are now compared against CVs 33 to 64 of the DD with the POS or NEG values potentially increasing. The same new FEN is used for the second t-test. Figure 3 shows the general pattern of testing, with each arrow representing a TTUV between each pairing of samples.

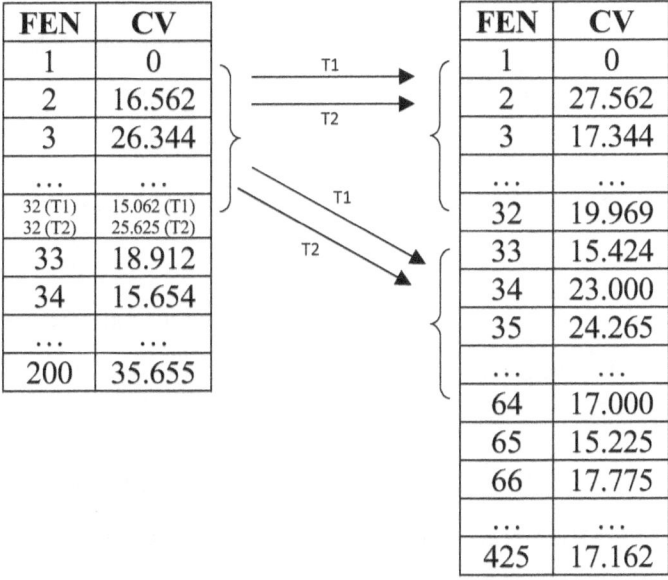

Figure 3: The t-tests between samples in the databases.

In the case of this example, the testing stops at the 416th CV of the DD since another chunk of 32 is not possible given its size. So, the first 32 CVs from the LD were tested 13 times against the DD. Testing then continues in the same way as explained but with the LD sample shifting to CVs 33 to 64. This second sample chunk of the LD is compared with all the sample chunks of the DD from the first one. The sample chunks for LD stop at the 192nd CV since another chunk of 32 is not possible given its size. The total number of TTUVs (for the first cycle) is therefore 6 x 2 x 13 = 156.

There will be a total of positive counts (POS) and negative counts (NEG) after all the statistical tests of all the samples from the two databases are completed in this first cycle. The ratio of the POS over the total counts, i.e. (POS + NEG) is returned as a percentage. So, if POS = 36 and NEG = 14, the value obtained is [36 / (36 + 14)] x 100 = 72%. This would be the 'ranking percentage' (RP) for the new FEN under consideration in this first cycle. The entire process is repeated for two more cycles with POS and NEG reset. The second cycle, however, must have a random sample size larger than the first but never exceeding 60.

One method of ensuring this over three cycles is to have a random sample size anywhere between 30 and 40 for the first cycle and for the remaining two cycles, an addition of a random number between 1 and 10 to determine the size of the new sample. For example, if '32' was selected as the first cycle's sample size, and then '5' was the random number to be added, the sample size for the second cycle would be, 32 + 5 = 37. For the third cycle, if '9' was selected at random, the third cycle's sample size for the databases would be, 37 + 9 = 45. This incremental sample size pushes the learning toward a more stable statistical result without becoming too large (even though larger samples do speed up the process). In the end, the average rank percentage (ARP) is used.

This could mean, for instance, (72% + 64% + 50%) / 3 = 62%. This value of 62% would be attributed to that single new FEN under consideration. One that is perhaps part of a larger collection that the solver has not seen yet. All of this is no doubt time consuming computationally as hundreds, if not thousands, of TTUVs are run in order to attribute a value to a single FEN so it can be ranked. On the other hand, if there was only one new FEN that needed to be decided upon, its ARP (e.g. 62%) would be on the favorable side since it is above 50%. This means the solver might want to take a look at it. Had it been equal to or below 50%, the solver might just want to skip it.

Chapter 4

Ranking and the General Algorithm

As explained in the previous chapter, the 'average rank percentage' (ARP) can be obtained for every new composition (with a FEN to represent its starting position). Assuming 10, 20 or even 100 new compositions are tested, they can all be ranked in descending order, i.e. with the highest ARPs naturally toward the top of the list. The idea is that more of what the solver is probably going to like will appear toward the top of such a list than we would expect from random chance. This kind of ranking matters because it is virtually impossible to predict with certainty which of the new compositions a particular solver is going to like. Even they cannot say for certain until seeing them.

Preference or taste also tends to change with time so a solver might suddenly come across something of a type they would not have liked before or decided now to like something of a type they perhaps did not appreciate as much before. Therefore, anything that increases the chances of the solver encountering a composition they will like in a given period of time can be helpful. This is precisely what a ranked list of compositions produced using the proposed machine learning method accomplishes. Table 3 shows what such a list might look like.

New Composition FEN	ARP
8/8/2Q5/1b6/1r6/5B2/k1N5/2K5 w - - 0 1	99.21
8/5K1k/8/8/7N/1p6/8/B7 w - - 0 1	97.56
3K4/6Rr/8/5B2/2Q5/8/8/3bk3 w - - 0 1	96.90
6Q1/8/8/1R5B/8/6R1/1Pp4K/1k6 w - - 0 1	93.89
1r6/8/6P1/1p1R4/k4N2/3p4/P5K1/2Q5 w - - 0 1	85.96
8/5R2/1k5K/2N2NR1/8/8/1p6/8 w - - 0 1	81.15
6R1/8/2K5/k7/8/3p4/1P6/8 w - - 0 1	73.61

Table 3: Example list of new compositions with their ARPs.

The particular FENs in Table 3 are not actually ranked this way but used here just to illustrate that a set of new composition FENs will have average rank percentages associated with them. Given a collection of perhaps 30 of these (only seven are shown in Table 3), if the solver would genuinely have liked only 10 of them (without any knowledge of their rankings), it is expected 7 or 8 would typically be found in the top 15 of the 30 new compositions ranked, when only 5 would be expected under normal circumstances (e.g. random selection).

This is actually a 40-60% improvement. It means that in going through such a collection of ranked compositions, the solver is more likely to find significantly more of what they will like and sooner. The solver's time and energy are therefore saved given that only the top half of the collection would need to be viewed in order to find most of what they would have ended up liking. The proposed method can be described in pseudocode as follows.

```
For a = 1 to 3 (i.e. cycles)
    Choose a sample size between 30 and 40 randomly (i.e. chunk size)
    For b = first chunk of 'liked' DB to last chunk of 'liked' DB
        For c = first chunk of 'disliked' DB to last chunk of 'disliked' DB
            For d = 1 to 2
                If d = 2 then
                    Replace last FEN in 'liked' sample with new FEN
                    Calculate and update the last 'change value' (CV)
                End If
                Compare 'liked' sample against 'disliked' sample using t-test
                Store t-test result
                If d = 2 then
                    Compare t-test result (of d = 1) against result (of d = 2)
                    If insignificant to significant then POS = POS + 1
                    If significant to insignificant then NEG = NEG + 1
                    Reset last FEN & CV in 'liked' sample to original values
                End If
            Next d
        Next c
    Next b
    Store rank percentage, i.e. [(POS) / (POS + NEG)] x 100
    Add random number between 1 and 10 to sample size
    POS = 0, NEG = 0
Next a
Return average rank percentage
```

This is done for each new FEN for which a determination needs to be made if it is likely to be 'liked' or 'disliked' by the solver. 'Appendix A' includes actual Microsoft Visual Basic code of the various functions necessary to make this work. Analogous code can be produced in virtually any modern programming language. Note that in computer programming, there are often ways to code the same things more efficiently depending on your skill level and what the language of choice is capable of.

Chapter 5

Experimental Results

I used collections of computer-generated chess problems by Chesthetica, an automatic chess problem composer (Chesthetica, 2020), divided into two PGN (Portable Game Notation) databases, i.e. 'liked' and 'disliked'. A PGN database is a standard format that allows chess positions and move sequences to be recorded. Figure 4 shows a partial PGN database of two compositions.

```
[Event "CGCP 02156"]
[Site "Selangor, MAS"]
[Date "2018.6.17 9:32:57 AM"]
[White "Chesthetica v10.67"]
[Black "Chesthetica v10.67"]
[Result "1-0"]
[FEN "7Q/8/3B4/8/8/2p2K2/2k1P3/8 w - - 0 1"]

1. Qb8 Kc1 2. Ba3+ Kd2 3. Qb1 c2 4. Bb4# 1-0

[Event "CGCP 02157"]
[Site "Selangor, MAS"]
[Date "2018.6.17 2:15:59 PM"]
[White "Chesthetica v10.67"]
[Black "Chesthetica v10.67"]
[Result "1-0"]
[FEN "4k3/N7/3P2P1/RK1P1p2/6n1/5nr1/8/8 w - - 0 1"]

1. Nc6 Nd4+ 2. Nxd4 Ne5 3. Ra8+ Kd7 4. Ra7+ Kxd6 5. Nxf5+ Kxd5 6. Nxg3 Nxg6 7. Nf5 Ke4 8. Ne7 Nf4 9. Kc4 Nd3 10. Nc6 Nb2+ 11. Kc3 Nd1+ 12. Kd2 Nf2 13. Ra4+ 1-0
```

Figure 4: Two compositions in a PGN database.

The first happens to be a forced mate in 4 and the second a '*White to Play and Win*' study. The 'liked' database (LD) consisted of 3,041 compositions generated between 20th July 2010 and 4th September 2020 that had been seen and selected by me. The 'disliked' database (DD) consisted of 10,028 compositions generated between 20th March 2020 and 4th September 2020 that had been seen and rejected by the me.

This does not mean that the DD contained invalid compositions but rather that I simply did not have a personal preference or particular liking for them. Quite often, other people in chess-playing and composing communities worldwide have been known to like compositions I do not and vice versa. Also, there were many low-quality compositions (in my opinion) intentionally generated as byproducts of unrelated experimental work which is why the DD used here happens to be so much larger within a shorter period. The databases were the largest I could obtain based on availability at the time. The most recent 20 compositions from the LD were used as the 'new and unseen' sample (NUS).

These had actually already been seen and preferred by me prior to any research work on this topic but they could serve as a good representation of a new and unseen collection for testing purposes. The LD and DD are sorted based on the dates and times the compositions were automatically generated (starting with the earliest). The aforementioned 20 happened to start from 15th

August 2020, 8:47 pm. The remaining 3,021 compositions, with the last composition generated just prior to that date and time, would thus be used to learn from using the proposed method. The LD was therefore truncated at that point. The same was done to the DD at composition 9,331 because everything up to that point was generated prior to the selection of the NUS compositions. This would also be used in the learning process.

For the interested reader, 'Appendix B' includes the first 500 entries of each, i.e. from the aforementioned 3,021 and 9,331 collections. Note that the FENs and change values are sufficient. So, for both the LD and DD, only compositions prior to all in the NUS should be used for learning. From the remaining 697 in the original DD (i.e. 9,332 to 10,028), 60 were selected at random and then divided sequentially and equally into three samples of 20 as 'baseline rejected' samples (in contrast to the NUS). I labeled them as BRS A, B and C. These represent analogously 'unseen' compositions but actually already seen and rejected by me prior to any research work on this topic. An algorithmic random number generator (internal to the Microsoft Visual Basic 6 programming language) was used for all random number generation purposes.

Random selection is actually not a necessity here given that all of the remaining 697 are from the DD, i.e. 60 compositions could have just as well been selected sequentially from any point early enough there. Table 4 shows the rank percentage (RP) score for each cycle for each FEN or position in the NUS, including the 'average rank percentage' (ARP) in the final column. The random but increasing sample sizes for each cycle (refer chapter 3) were not recorded because they are not relevant here.

FEN	Cycle 1	Cycle 2	Cycle 3	Average
1	90.20	80.91	88.71	86.60
2	63.33	50.96	71.01	61.77
3	75.63	70.93	78.72	75.09
4	80.98	83.50	83.56	82.68
5	14.17	16.04	17.11	15.77
6	97.57	96.83	95.29	96.56
7	60.43	78.26	60.61	66.43
8	52.50	62.89	47.22	54.20
9	0.45	6.08	6.90	4.48
10	76.88	71.91	67.86	72.22
11	38.97	40.00	39.44	39.47
12	68.71	78.05	65.08	70.61
13	61.81	58.33	50.00	56.71
14	44.44	51.81	55.22	50.49
15	31.62	46.59	26.56	34.93
16	95.37	99.21	92.47	95.69
17	97.67	94.12	94.44	95.41
18	4.23	12.34	14.29	10.29
19	73.04	86.81	70.31	76.72
20	51.39	58.33	55.56	55.09

Table 4: The RPs for the 'new and unseen' sample (and the ARP).

The first hypothesis is that using the proposed novel machine learning method, more of the NUS would be selected for compared to the three BRS ones, based only on what was learned from the 'liked' and 'disliked' compositions prior to them. The second hypothesis is that a statistically significant difference would exist between the mean ARP of the NUS compared to the mean ARP of each of the three BRS ones, with the former always being higher. Analogous data for the BRS ones, but showing just the ARPs, are in Table 5.

FEN	BRS A	BRS B	BRS C
1	73.49	34.99	1.65
2	73.86	17.82	34.69
3	26.22	20.15	38.14
4	6.33	24.57	93.01
5	30.37	4.36	0.71
6	67.27	15.14	25.33
7	7.73	5.46	21.16
8	28.65	34.03	36.63
9	7.98	8.68	6.17
10	77.62	98.43	38.65
11	6.35	39.93	2.91
12	55.01	5.13	62.66
13	14.51	46.62	4.18
14	13.02	19.85	6.14
15	89.76	35.88	3.36
16	52.69	60.62	70.48
17	49.77	56.87	29.75
18	18.53	82.48	8.60
19	28.50	29.24	85.58
20	67.15	34.09	2.69

Table 5: The ARPs for the baseline rejected samples.

Comparing the NUS against each of the three baseline rejected samples using a two-tailed, two-sample t-test assuming unequal variances (TTUV) at a significance level of 0.05, the means were always different to a statistically significant degree, with the mean ARP for the NUS being significantly higher. Table 6 shows the result of each comparison (the mean ARP for the sample is in brackets).

	NUS (60.06)
BRS A (39.74)	t(38) = 2.308, p = 0.027
BRS B (33.72)	t(38) = 3.134, p = 0.003
BRS C (28.62)	t(38) = 3.494, p = 0.001

Table 6: T-test results of the NUS compared against BRS.

The ARPs of the FENs in the NUS (rightmost column in Table 4) were then combined with the ARPs of the FENs for each BRS (columns 2, 3 and 4 in Table 5). So, there were three columns of 40 ARPs, each one having the ARPs of the NUS in them. Sorted from highest to lowest, the associated FENs in the NUS appeared in the top half with respect to BRS A, B and C as follows: 13/20 (65%), 15/20 (75%) and 16/20 (80%), respectively. Overall, between 65% and 80% of the time (averaging 73.33%), which is well above random chance where only 10/20 or 50% would be expected. To be sure, I repeated the experiment.

This time, however, the second most recent 20 compositions from the LD (i.e. 3,002 to 3,021) were used as the second 'new and unseen' sample (NUS2). They happened to start from 31st July 2020, 2:44 pm. The earlier 3,001 compositions would therefore be used to learn from. The DD was truncated at composition 6,287 because this is the point just prior to when the compositions in NUS2 were generated.

From the remaining 3,741 in the DD (i.e. 6,288 to 10,028), 60 were selected at random, as before, and then divided into three samples of 20 as the second set of 'baseline rejected' samples. I labeled them as BRS2 A, B and C. The ARPs are shown in Table 7. 'Appendix C' contains all the NUS and BRS composition positions from both experiments as diagrams.

FEN	NUS2	BRS2 A	BRS2 B	BRS2 C
1	49.69	16.52	43.37	30.68
2	54.27	6.52	8.55	40.86
3	33.58	1.47	10.03	14.86
4	35.31	12.22	80.73	4.50
5	67.03	67.53	82.26	27.98
6	68.59	75.71	97.13	78.80
7	69.97	49.45	47.38	10.65
8	79.65	13.76	23.70	53.78
9	71.05	5.05	2.64	90.76
10	52.56	6.19	99.59	50.07
11	80.23	15.70	45.47	5.05
12	91.45	14.23	22.44	28.16
13	89.62	7.09	24.70	9.78
14	33.38	23.74	4.21	7.16
15	85.41	12.53	2.45	12.16
16	99.74	2.14	11.50	55.51
17	68.41	13.37	79.36	75.86
18	88.36	10.90	4.00	6.30
19	13.65	8.81	8.94	12.71
20	32.92	15.38	5.30	6.00

Table 7: The ARPs for the repeated experiment.

Comparing the NUS2 against each of the three baseline rejected samples, the means were always different to a statistically significant degree, with the mean ARP for the NUS2 being significantly higher. Table 8 shows the result of each comparison (the mean ARP for the sample is in brackets).

	NUS2 (63.24)
BRS2 A (18.92)	$t(37) = 6.248, p < 0.001$
BRS2 B (35.19)	$t(34) = 2.989, p = 0.005$
BRS2 C (31.08)	$t(37) = 3.930, p < 0.001$

Table 8: T-test results of the NUS2 compared against BRS2.

Sorted from highest to lowest, the associated FENs in the NUS2 appeared in the top half with respect to BRS2 A, B and C as follows: 17/20 (85%), 15/20 (75%) and 14/20 (70%), respectively. Overall, between 70% and 85% of the time (averaging 76.67%), which is also well above random chance, just like the previous experiment. Combining both results, the average is 75%.

In practice, this means that once new FENs are analyzed (and ranked from highest to lowest) based on what the computer has learned from existing 'liked' and 'disliked' selections, the solver is more likely to be able to find ones they prefer sooner than otherwise, i.e. typically 75% in just the top half, equivalent to a performance increase of 50% compared to a regular case of no learning being applied to the new and unseen compositions.

Chapter 6

Conclusions

The experimental results presented in the previous section demonstrate that the proposed novel machine learning method is indeed able to learn from existing single user preference data, at least in the domain of chess problems. Note that the change from one object to another (see chapter 2), in this case chess positions in the FEN format, has nothing to do with the actual rules of chess but merely the shift from one kind of byte-length character data to another kind (e.g. 'Q' to 'K', '1' to 'b'). This suggests the learning method could also be applied to images or other types of objects with discrete components, perhaps with some modifications or adaptations; but this is beyond the scope of this book.

The way the 'change values' between objects are processed implies that the ordering of the objects, i.e. which one comes first, second, third etc. can influence the end result, even though at present this has not been specifically tested for. The learning should therefore be sensitive to how a user's preferences may (and likely will) change over time. The incremental yet random size selection of the samples to be used introduces some variability into the process but this is stabilized by utilizing the average rank percentage over three cycles of hundreds, if not thousands of t-tests between the samples for each new FEN under consideration.

Even these are flexible aspects of the method that can be modified or adapted to suit particular domains or needs. For example, a fixed but much larger sample size could be used to speed up the process given large databases of user preference data (i.e. liked and disliked material), in which case only one cycle may be necessary, speeding it up even further. On the other hand, doing so may not work as well as the present approach just described; so, it is up to interested readers or researchers to test for themselves what settings appear to work most reliably in their domains of investigation. Under typical conditions, as was the case here, processing can indeed take many hours.

For instance, 1,000 new and unseen positions processed using a standard desktop computer with user preference databases of about the sizes in our experiments (see chapter 5) could take around 24 hours to complete or between one and two full minutes per position. This would still be considered worthwhile, however, since the system could be run in the back-ground while other work is being done. It would save significant amounts of time and energy on the part of the user by not having to go through all 1,000 of those new positions manually but only 500 or so to obtain most of what they would have liked. Given that there are limits to human time and energy, large collections of new and unseen objects are seldom fully and properly assessed anyway.

In many cases they are either completely rejected or only a small portion is examined; even then probably less thoroughly as time passes given that most humans tend to tire or bore fairly quickly anyway (McSpadden, 2015). The automatic sorting of the new objects (assuming more than one is being evaluated) based on their average rank percentages can easily be performed computationally after the process ends so the method is essentially something that can be set and forgotten about until it completes. It does not require much involvement by the user once it is running. As mentioned earlier, the proposed method uses single user preference data and that means it does not rely on external (i.e. other) user preference data or any personal details about the user to be matched with 'other users like them'.

Aside from the selection and classification of earlier objects as being 'liked' or 'disliked', nothing else from the user is required. User privacy is also better guarded as the machine learning does not require sharing information (it can be done locally on one's own computer using one's own data). It is not yet known what the minimum sizes of the 'liked' and 'disliked' databases should be but since statistical testing is a major component of the proposed method, presumably the larger they are the better. The downside is that the overall process will take longer as these sizes increase. For that reason, the quality of data is important. I suggest that for these databases, only the objects that have actually been seen and properly evaluated by the user be collected. Ambiguous or undecided objects should be avoided and not included.

As time goes by, perhaps some of the earliest objects need not even be included anymore since the user's taste or preferences may have changed significantly enough. Subsets of about the sizes used in our experiments or smaller can be randomly selected from both databases if faster processing time is a critical issue. The optimal sample and database sizes in any particular domain, including chess problems, has yet to be determined experimentally, however. This is also worthy of further inquiry. At this point, it remains unclear how the method 'learns' from the 'change values' between objects since they have nothing to do with the actual rules of chess. Our best guess is that there are sufficiently-detectable 'patterns', invisible to humans, that emerge through this process from the databases. Patterns that can be disrupted by new chess problems that somehow do not 'fit' with them, despite a margin of error.

Each pattern would therefore theoretically also be unique to each user and even changes as they change. It is a fascinating idea worthy of further investigation in itself but again, beyond the scope of this book. Another aspect that might be of interest to some is the nature of what is being learned. Even within the domain of chess compositions, is it the aesthetics, the difficulty, the complexity or something else? Our best estimation of the answer is that it captures, to a reasonably good extent, an amalgamation of all that and more, including the 'intangible' and unquantifiable aspects of why individual users like and dislike as they do. The patterns mentioned earlier may be analogous to paths and points in a long and continuing journey that are invisible from the perspective of the one walking (they are making complex yet 'lower-level' decisions of their own from where they stand) yet from a bird's-eye view there is a general but unique pattern to their choices. A kind of swarm intelligence (Schranz et al., 2021), if you will, but involving just a single agent.

Finally, note that this is a novel machine learning approach and still requires more testing (e.g. contrasting learning performance based on many users), even within the domain of chess composition. It may be a challenge to obtain reliable 'liked' and 'disliked' databases of sufficient sizes for single users in most domains, however, and this is a limitation worth pointing out as well. In this book, I have merely presented the general method itself and some experimental results obtained. Regardless of what other researchers may find, I am actually currently using this method within this domain for my own purposes because it does indeed seem to work. It is my hope that I have documented it well enough for researchers or interested parties to try for themselves using their own user preference data, and perhaps even improve upon it in ways I cannot yet imagine at this point.

REFERENCES

Associated Press, The (2016). *Google DeepMind Computer AlphaGo Sweeps Human Champ in Go Matches,* CBC News, 12 March. https://www.cbc.ca/news/technology/go-google-alphago-lee-sedol-deepmind-1.3488913 (accessed 18 October 2020).

Chesthetica (2020). *The World's Most Advanced Automatic Chess Problem Composer.* http://www.chesthetica.com (accessed 21 October 2020).

Chiu, A. (2019). *A Chess Grandmaster's Success was 'Unreal.' Until He was Caught in the Bathroom with a Phone*, The Washington Post, July 15. https://www.washingtonpost.com/nation/2019/07/15/chess-grandmasters-success-was-unreal-then-he-was-caught-bathroom-with-phone (accessed 18 October 2020).

Deldjoo, Y., Schedl, M., Cremonesi, P. and Pasi, G. (2020). Recommender Systems Leveraging Multimedia Content, *ACM Computing Surveys (CSUR)*, 53(5), pp. 1-38.

Dhou, K. (2008). *Chess Software and its Impact on Chess Players*, Master of Science Thesis, University of Northern British Columbia. DOI: https://doi.org/10.24124/2008/bpgub1368 (accessed 18 October 2020).

Friedel, F. (2017). *Famous Chess Player Arrested in Bulgaria*, ChessBase News, Hamburg, Germany, 22 March. https://en.chessbase.com/post/famous-chess-player-arrested-in-bulgaria (accessed 18 October 2020).

Friedel, F. (2018). *Solution to a Truly Remarkable Study*, ChessBase News, Hamburg, Germany, 12 February. https://en.chessbase.com/post/solution-to-a-truly-remarkable-study (accessed 18 October 2020).

Howard, K. (1967). *The Enjoyment of Chess Problems*, Dover Publications, 4th Edition, New York, N.Y., USA.

Hsu, F-H. (2002). *Behind Deep Blue: Building the Computer that Defeated the World Chess Champion*, Princeton University Press, USA.

Iqbal, A. (2019). *Computationally Estimating the Solvability of Forced Mate Sequences*, Figshare, York Way, London, United Kingdom, 25 June, DOI: 10.6084/m9.figshare.8319881. https://figshare.com/articles/Computationally_Estimating_the_Solvability_of_Forced_Mate_Sequences/8319881 (accessed 18 October 2020).

Khadilkar, D. (2019). *Preparing Against your Opponent's Favourite Variation*, ChessBase News, Hamburg, Germany, 5 August. https://en.chessbase.com/post/preparing-against-your-opponent-s-favourite-variation (accessed 18 October 2020).

Khenissi, S., Mariem, B. and Nasraoui, O. (2020). *Theoretical Modeling of the Iterative Properties of User Discovery in a Collaborative Filtering Recommender System*, in Fourteenth ACM Conference on Recommender Systems, September, pp. 348-357.

Levitt, J. and Friedgood D. (2008). *Secrets of Spectacular Chess*, 2nd Edition (Expanded), 1 May, Everyman Chess, London, England. ISBN: 978-1857445510.

Margulies, S. (1977). Principles of Beauty, *Psychological Reports*, Vol. 41, pp. 3-11.

McSpadden, K. (2015). *You Now Have a Shorter Attention Span than a Goldfish*, Time Magazine, 14 May, https://time.com/3858309/attention-spans-goldfish (accessed on 21 October 2020).

Metz, C. (2016). In Two Moves, AlphaGo and Lee Sedol Redefined the Future, *Wired*, 16 March. https://www.wired.com/2016/03/two-moves-alphago-lee-sedol-redefined-future (accessed 18 October 2020).

Newborn, M. (2011). *Beyond Deep Blue: Chess in the Stratosphere*, Springer, 2011th Edition, ISBN-13 : 978-0857293404.

Rai, A. K. and Dwivedi, R. K. (2020). *Fraud Detection in Credit Card Data using Unsupervised Machine Learning Based Scheme*, in 2020 International Conference on Electronics and Sustainable Communication Systems (ICESC), 2-4 July, pp. 421-426, IEEE.

Samuel, A. L. (1959). Some Studies in Machine Learning Using the Game of Checkers, *IBM Journal of Research and Development,* 44: 206-226.

Schranz, M., Di Caro, G. A., Schmickl, T., Elmenreich, W., Arvin, F., Şekercioğlu, A. and Sende, M. (2021). Swarm Intelligence and Cyber-physical Systems: Concepts, Challenges and Future Trends, *Swarm and Evolutionary Computation*, Vol. 60, February, Article 100762 (in progress).

Shenk, D. (2006). *The Immortal Game: A History of Chess*, Doubleday, Random House Inc., New York, USA. ISBN: 978-0385510103.

Silver, D., Hubert, T., Schrittwieser, J., Antonoglou, I., Lai, M., Guez, A., Lanctot, M., Sifre, L., Kumaran, D., Graepel, T., Lillicrap, T., Simonyan, K., and Hassabis, D. (2018). A General Reinforcement Learning Algorithm that Masters Chess, Shogi, and Go through Self-play, *Science*, 362 (6419), pp. 1140-1144.

Wikipedia (2020). *Forsyth-Edwards Notation*, https://en.wikipedia.org/wiki/Forsyth–Edwards_Notation (accessed 19 October 2020).

Yan, S. (2016). A Google Computer Victorious Over the World's 'Go' Champion, CNN Money. https://money.cnn.com/2016/03/12/technology/google-deepmind-alphago-wins (accessed 18 October 2020).

Zhuang, F., Qi, Z., Duan, K., Xi, D., Zhu, Y., Zhu, H., Xiong, H. and He, Q. (2020). A Comprehensive Survey on Transfer Learning, Proceedings of the IEEE, July, pp. 1-34.

Appendix A

Programming Code Examples

The following are actual Microsoft Visual Basic 6 code examples (with commentary) related to the novel machine learning method proposed in this book. They contain more details than algorithmic steps, for the interested reader or software developer. The first function accepts a Forsyth-Edwards Notation (FEN) string and returns its 'expanded' version.

```
Private Function Expand_FEN(the_fen As String) As String
'e.g. "8/8/2Q5/1b6/1r6/5B2/k1N5/2K5 w - - 0 1" will return
"11111111/11111111/11Q11111/1b111111/1r111111/5B11/k1N11111/11K11111 w - - 0 1"

Dim arlines() As String, i As Integer, j As Integer, k As Integer, new_fen As String

arlines() = Split(the_fen, "/")

For i = 0 To UBound(arlines)
    For j = 1 To Len(arlines(i))
        If IsDigit(Mid(arlines(i), j, 1)) = True Then
            For k = 1 To Val(Mid(arlines(i), j, 1))
                new_fen = new_fen & "1"
```

```
            Next k
        Else
            new_fen = new_fen & Mid(arlines(i), j, 1)
        End If
    Next j
    new_fen = new_fen & "/"
Next i

Expand_FEN = Mid(new_fen, 1, Len(new_fen) - 1)

End Function
```

The next function accepts the output of 'Expand_FEN' above and returns just the necessary segment with the slashes removed (as explained in chapter 2).

```
Private Function Essential_FEN_Data(expanded_FEN As
String) As String
'e.g.
"11111111/11111111/11Q11111/1b111111/1r111111/5B11/k1N1111
1/11K11111 w - - 0 1" will return
"111111111111111111Q111111b1111111r1111115B11k1N1111111K11
111"

Dim i As Integer, ess_fen As String

For i = 1 To Len(expanded_FEN)
    If Mid(expanded_FEN, i, 1) = " " Then Exit For
    If Mid(expanded_FEN, i, 1) <> "/" Then
        ess_fen = ess_fen & Mid(expanded_FEN, i, 1)
    End If
```

```
Next i

Essential_FEN_Data = ess_fen

End Function
```

The following is for the two-sample t-test assuming unequal variances (TTUV). The two samples (of 'change values') are passed to this function 'by reference' because in many programming languages, arrays cannot be passed 'by value'. This means the original values or memory locations will be accessed instead of just copies of them. This function may be included under a larger 'statistical' module or class.

```
Public Function TTUV(ByRef sample1() As Double, ByRef sample2() As Double) As Double
'two-sample t-test assuming unequal variances
'the t_stat value needs to be greater than the critical value to be statistically significant (otherwise '0' is returned)

Dim t_stat As Double, s1mean As Double, s2mean As Double, s1size As Double, s2size As Double, s1var As Double, s2var As Double, df As Double
Dim df_num As Double, df_den As Double

s1mean = Stats.Mean(sample1): s2mean = Stats.Mean(sample2)
s1size = UBound(sample1) + 1: s2size = UBound(sample2) + 1
s1var = Stats.Variance(sample1)
s2var = Stats.Variance(sample2)
```

```
t_stat = (s1mean - s2mean) / Sqr((s1var / s1size) + (s2var
/ s2size))
df_num = ((s1var / s1size) + (s2var / s2size)) ^ 2
df_den = (((s1var / s1size) ^ 2) / (s1size - 1)) +
(((s2var / s2size) ^ 2) / (s2size - 1))
df = Int(Round(df_num / df_den))

If t_stat > Crit_Value(CInt(df)) Then
    TTUV = Round(t_stat, 3)
Else
'not significant
    TTUV = 0
End If

End Function
```

The one below is the associated 'critical value' function needed by the one above. The t-table (for the t-distribution) is stored externally as a text file in this case. The values could also be 'hard-coded' internally.

```
Public Function Crit_Value(df_val As Integer) As Double
'returns the two-tailed critical value for the t-
distribution based on a default alpha value of '0.05'

Static strtext As String
Dim arlines1() As String, arlines2() As String, i As
Integer

If strtext = vbNullString Then strtext =
Main.File_to_Text(app.Path & "\" & "t_table.txt")
```

```
arlines1 = Split(strtext, vbNewLine)

If df_val > 100 Then df_val = 100
'it defaults to the last value if greater than available
in the list

For i = 0 To UBound(arlines1)
    If arlines1(i) <> vbNullString Then
        arlines2 = Split(arlines1(i), vbTab)
        If arlines2(0) = df_val Then
            Crit_Value = Round(Val(arlines2(1)), 3)
            Exit Function
        End If
    End If
Next i

End Function
```

Next is the 'FEN Change Value' function which calculates and returns the 'change value' between two FENs passed to it.

```
Private Function FEN_Change_Value(last_fen As String,
current_fen As String) As Double
'in the standard format exported by Essential_FEN_Data
'short examples: '11111' changes to '11Q11' is a 1/5 * 100
= 20% change; '11Q11' to '11K11' is a 1/5 * 50 = 10%
change; '11K11' to 'B1R1N' is a 2/5 * 100 + 1/5 * 50 = 40
+ 10 = 50% change

Dim i As Integer, fen_len As Integer, lfcc As String, cfcc
As String, multiplier As Double, tpc As Double
```

```
fen_len = Len(last_fen)


For i = 1 To fen_len
    lfcc = Mid(last_fen, i, 1)
    'last fen current character
    cfcc = Mid(current_fen, i, 1)
    'current fen current character

    If cfcc = "1" Xor lfcc = "1" Then
    'any character (e.g. 'Q', 'K') changing to '1'
    (default blank state) or vice versa is a 100% change
        multiplier = 100
    Else
    'change to a non-default state (e.g. 'Q' to 'K')
        If cfcc <> lfcc Then
        'if both are '1' then nothing happens (no change)
        'if both are say, 'Q' and 'Q', then nothing
        happens either
            multiplier = 50
        End If
    End If

    If cfcc <> lfcc Then tpc = tpc + ((1 / fen_len) *
    multiplier)
    'the total (percentage) change value
Next i

FEN_Change_Value = tpc

End Function
```

Finally, we have the main machine learning function that accepts a new position (FEN) to be evaluated against the 'liked' and 'disliked' databases provided by the user. This is only for one cycle, however. The function will have to be invoked three times to get the average (a new random sample size specified each time).

```
Private Function ML_Analysis(new_fen As String,
sample_size As Integer) As Double
'statistically analyzes the 'liked' and 'disliked' DBs
'it accepts the new FEN to be tested against them and
generates a probability score

Static liked_str As String, dliked_str As String
Dim liked_cv() As String, dliked_cv() As String
Dim liked() As String, disliked() As String
Dim liked_fen() As String, dliked_fen() As String,
liked_temp() As String, dliked_temp() As String
Dim liked_size As Double, dliked_size As Double, i As
Double, j As Double, k As Double, l As Double
Dim liked_ta() As Double, dliked_ta() As Double, liked_lb
As Double, dliked_lb As Double, the_sample_size As Integer
Dim liked_rounds As Double, dliked_rounds As Double,
ttuv_output As String, backup_val As Double, ttuvr As
Double, new_ttuvr As Double, neg As Double, pos As Double,
liked_ls As String, liked_sls As String, rand_ls As Double

the_sample_size = sample_size

If liked_str = vbNullString Then
    liked_str = File_to_Text(app.Path & "\" &
    "Liked_DB.txt")
```

```vb
        dliked_str = File_to_Text(app.Path & "\" & _
        "Dliked_DB.txt")
        'reads the data in these files
    End If


    liked = Split(liked_str, vbNewLine)
    disliked = Split(dliked_str, vbNewLine)

    ReDim liked_cv(0 To UBound(liked))
    ReDim liked_fen(0 To UBound(liked))
    ReDim dliked_cv(0 To UBound(disliked))
    ReDim dliked_fen(0 To UBound(disliked))

    For i = 0 To UBound(liked)
        If liked(i) <> vbNullString Then
            liked_temp = Split(liked(i), vbTab)
            liked_fen(i) = liked_temp(0)
            liked_cv(i) = liked_temp(1)
            'obtains the FEN strings and the change values
        End If
    Next i

    For i = 0 To UBound(disliked)
        If disliked(i) <> vbNullString Then
            dliked_temp = Split(disliked(i), vbTab)
            dliked_fen(i) = dliked_temp(0)
            dliked_cv(i) = dliked_temp(1)
        End If
    Next i

    liked_size = UBound(liked) - 1
    dliked_size = UBound(disliked) - 1
```

```
the_sample_size = the_sample_size - 1
'a size of 30 means array indices 0 through 29


dliked_rounds = Int(dliked_size / (the_sample_size + 1))
liked_rounds = Int(liked_size / (the_sample_size + 1))


ReDim liked_ta(0 To the_sample_size)
ReDim dliked_ta(0 To the_sample_size)


liked_lb = 0: dliked_lb = 0
'the lower bounds for each sample


For i = 1 To liked_rounds
    For j = 0 To the_sample_size
        liked_ta(j) = Val(liked_cv(liked_lb + j))
        'the liked temp array stores a 'chunk' of values
        from the full array
    Next j

    liked_sls = liked_fen((i * (the_sample_size + 1)) - 2)
    'second last slot
    liked_ls = liked_fen((i * (the_sample_size + 1)) - 1)
    'last slot
    backup_val = liked_ta(the_sample_size)

    For k = 1 To dliked_rounds
        For l = 0 To the_sample_size
            dliked_ta(l) = Val(dliked_cv(dliked_lb +
            l))
        Next l

        ttuvr = Stats.TTUV(liked_ta, dliked_ta)
```

```
                'gets the TTUV result for this pairing of chunks


                liked_ta(the_sample_size) =
                Round(FEN_Change_Value(Essential_FEN_Data(Exp
                and_FEN(liked_sls)),
                Essential_FEN_Data(Expand_FEN(new_fen))), 3)


                new_ttuvr = Stats.TTUV(liked_ta, dliked_ta)
                'a new TTUV value is obtained

                If ttuvr <> 0 Then
                    If new_ttuvr = 0 Then neg = neg + 1
                Else
                    If new_ttuvr <> 0 Then pos = pos + 1
                End If


                liked_ta(the_sample_size) = backup_val
                dliked_lb = dliked_lb + (the_sample_size + 1)
            Next k

            dliked_lb = 0
            liked_lb = liked_lb + (the_sample_size + 1)
            DoEvents
        Next i

        If (pos + neg) > 0 Then
            ML_Analysis = (pos / (pos + neg)) * 100
        Else
            ML_Analysis = 0
        End If

    End Function
```

Appendix B

Database Entries

The following are the first 500 entries in the 'liked database' (LD) and 'disliked database' (DD) used in the experiment (see chapter 5). On the left is the FEN and on the right is the 'change value' (CV) compared to the previous FEN. The first CV defaults to '0'.

Liked Database

FEN	CV
8/8/2Q5/1b6/1r6/5B2/k1N5/2K5 w - - 0 1	0
8/5K1k/8/8/7N/1p6/8/B7 w - - 0 1	18.75
3K4/6Rr/8/5B2/2Q5/8/8/3bk3 w - - 0 1	16.406
6Q1/8/8/1R5B/8/6R1/1Pp4K/1k6 w - - 0 1	23.438
1r6/8/6P1/1p1R4/k4N2/3p4/P5K1/2Q5 w - - 0 1	25.781
8/5R2/1k5K/2N2NR1/8/8/1p6/8 w - - 0 1	26.562
6R1/8/2K5/k7/8/3p4/1P6/8 w - - 0 1	16.406
8/8/8/3pQ3/1N6/1K6/3k4/8 w - - 0 1	15.625
6k1/8/5Rp1/4B3/8/4K3/8/b6Q w - - 0 1	16.406
5B2/1q6/5Q2/5B1R/4N3/1k6/8/1K6 w - - 0 1	21.094
K7/8/Q4p2/8/8/8/3P1N1B/2k5 w - - 0 1	21.094
8/3B4/7Q/2BN4/8/K2k4/8/1q6 w - - 0 1	21.875
8/1K1kP3/8/8/4B3/7p/8/4R3 w - - 0 1	17.969
5B2/8/5Q2/1k6/8/5p2/1N6/4K3 w - - 0 1	16.406
4R3/7b/5K2/5N1k/8/8/4P3/8 w - - 0 1	16.406
4R3/8/5p2/7K/1N1k4/8/8/2R5 w - - 0 1	10.938

1K4R1/3P4/1k6/8/8/8/8/8 w - - 0 1	15.625
8/6P1/8/1R5K/8/5Npk/8/8 w - - 0 1	15.625
4K3/8/3R4/6N1/8/p6N/8/7k w - - 0 1	16.406
k7/4n2B/8/8/8/8/K2b4/6Q1 w - - 0 1	18.75
8/1Nbpk3/6K1/8/3N1p2/5r2/8/3Q4 w - - 0 1	21.094
7k/8/2p1P1K1/1B6/q2b4/3P4/8/B7 w - - 0 1	22.656
4k3/8/5PN1/8/3Q4/8/2K1p3/8 w - - 0 1	18.75
N2k2q1/8/5N2/Kp6/b7/4Q3/8/8 w - - 0 1	19.531
1K6/1Q6/5k2/1p6/3P1N2/1p4B1/qp6/8 w - - 0 1	22.656
6B1/4Q3/3B3b/8/3k4/2p3K1/8/8 w - - 0 1	21.875
8/5Q2/8/7K/4N3/5n1k/5r1P/8 w - - 0 1	21.875
1R6/1p1k2P1/8/4K3/1B6/8/8/8 w - - 0 1	20.312
7k/5K2/p7/5BP1/8/r3b3/8/6B1 w - - 0 1	21.875
8/3Q4/8/3r4/3k4/3P2Q1/8/4K3 w - - 0 1	21.875
2b5/4k3/2Q5/8/7K/8/3B3R/8 w - - 0 1	18.75
4Qr2/r3P1R1/5NNk/6n1/6K1/8/8/2b5 w - - 0 1	24.219
8/5p1b/3K1k2/8/1B6/1n4Q1/8/8 w - - 0 1	25.781
k7/1r3Q2/8/8/8/1B6/5p1K/8 w - - 0 1	15.625
4b3/4n3/8/8/4R1K1/8/2BbRN2/2kN4 w - - 0 1	22.656
8/8/2b5/6B1/5p2/2K4Q/4Bk2/8 w - - 0 1	21.875
1Q3K2/8/R5p1/5kr1/4N3/8/8/8 w - - 0 1	19.531
8/8/3K3Q/8/k7/7p/N7/N7 w - - 0 1	20.312
8/7b/8/k7/2R5/2R5/1Rn5/2K5 w - - 0 1	20.312
8/4r3/6B1/8/q4k1K/8/5N2/Q3B3 w - - 0 1	23.438
k3N3/n7/RpP1K3/1r6/2N5/8/8/6Q1 w - - 0 1	28.125
5K2/8/2B5/4kp2/1R1p4/4P3/6N1/8 w - - 0 1	25.781
8/8/5N2/8/2r5/8/Q2p4/1r1k1K2 w - - 0 1	23.438
8/8/8/3R4/8/6K1/r5n1/5B1k w - - 0 1	15.625
8/Q3K3/6N1/5p1k/5R2/5P1q/8/8 w - - 0 1	21.875
3K2bk/4P2q/3BB3/3QR3/5p2/8/8/8 w - - 0 1	23.438
k4b2/8/K1b2n2/8/1Q6/8/8/8 w - - 0 1	25
8/1pPK4/8/krpN4/8/8/8/3B4 w - - 0 1	21.875
r7/4Q3/3N4/k6B/7K/8/8/8 w - - 0 1	18.75
2RQ4/3P4/8/8/3rP3/1B1k1K2/q1p1N3/4b3 w - - 0 1	28.125
8/1K6/8/kp6/8/1P2B3/4p3/N7 w - - 0 1	25
8/1R6/6n1/6p1/8/1B6/5K2/7k w - - 0 1	15.625

```
1B6/8/kp6/qN1n4/2P2Q2/8/3p3K/8 w - - 0 1                25
4K3/8/8/1N6/5n2/8/8/k1BR4 w - - 0 1                     19.531
4k3/6P1/3B1K1n/8/8/8/8/2R5 w - - 0 1                    14.062
1k1B2R1/bB4r1/1n1K4/8/8/1Q6/8/8 w - - 0 1               18.75
8/8/8/4R3/2K5/6p1/5N2/k7 w - - 0 1                      21.875
1nkn4/2Pp4/8/3N4/1BB5/3N4/8/6K1 w - - 0 1               21.094
2q2k1K/3pR1p1/3b4/6n1/8/B2BQ3/8/8 w - - 0 1             25
2b5/8/7N/5n2/8/8/R4K1k w - - 0 1                        24.219
8/8/4B3/1n2B3/8/8/4K2k w - - 0 1                        14.062
1N6/k2N4/3R4/8/4K3/8/p7/8 w - - 0 1                     17.188
7K/8/2B4k/2N5/8/4Rp2/8/8 w - - 0 1                      18.75
2K5/k1p5/2B5/B7/8/8/8/8 w - - 0 1                       14.062
8/4K1R1/5nBk/8/8/7N/1B1n4/8 w - - 0 1                   20.312
7B/8/8/3r4/8/3k4/5R2/3K1N2 w - - 0 1                    21.875
K7/3R4/4bkB1/3PNN2/3R4/8/8/8 w - - 0 1                  21.094
k7/n1B1N3/2R5/8/8/8/1K4p1/8 w - - 0 1                   22.656
8/4nkBK/8/1Q4PP/4r3/8/8/8 w - - 0 1                     21.094
8/5kpq/K1BPR1N1/4B3/p7/1rQ5/8/8 w - - 0 1               23.438
R2K1k2/2r1pB2/1N5P/8/8/8/8/8 w - - 0 1                  28.906
2QK4/8/3k4/3P2p1/8/5P2/8/8 w - - 0 1                    18.75
8/2N1Q3/6K1/8/2kp4/8/1P2b3/1B6 w - - 0 1                21.875
1B5b/3K4/5k2/8/5P2/8/8/4Q3 w - - 0 1                    21.875
2q1Nk2/5PN1/2p2B2/2K5/4R3/3p4/8/8 w - - 0 1             22.656
8/8/6Q1/2p2B2/3kb3/8/2PB4/2K5 w - - 0 1                 23.438
8/8/4R3/1K6/8/8/5P1p/3R1Nk1 w - - 0 1                   23.438
2k5/6K1/2NP4/3B4/3p4/3N4/8/b7 w - - 0 1                 23.438
8/K1p5/p4r2/3P1knP/6p1/2Q4N/8/3B2B1 w - - 0 1           30.469
k7/5P2/5p2/K3P3/4pr2/4P3/8/8 w - - 0 1                  30.469
1b6/8/8/4Q3/8/1bK5/8/1k6 w - - 0 1                      17.969
8/4R3/1k5B/8/1K1p4/5B1n/8/8 w - - 0 1                   18.75
7r/6PP/8/5K2/7k/8/6P1/8 w - - 0 1                       20.312
8/6R1/8/7K/8/8/pk6/b4R2 w - - 0 1                       16.406
8/8/8/8/8/3Br1R1/3b1k1K/4N3 w - - 0 1                   20.312
8/8/8/8/1b2QK2/k3N3/4R3 w - - 0 1                       15.625
3B4/3N1q2/1KP1k1B1/3rb3/8/3n1N2/8/8 w - - 0 1           24.219
1k6/N5r1/1BKn4/q7/8/8/1Q6/8 w - - 0 1                   25
```

5bb1/2nP1kp1/1K5R/8/8/5N2/8/8 w - - 0 1	21.875
K7/3B2P1/7p/2P4k/8/4np2/6R1/8 w - - 0 1	18.75
8/4N3/K7/2k5/1b6/1rP3B1/2N3rQ/8 w - - 0 1	25
NQBnk1K1/3bP3/7B/8/8/8/3r4/8 w - - 0 1	28.906
1B3k1K/4R2p/8/3N4/8/4b3/8/8 w - - 0 1	21.875
8/2K5/b7/1qB4R/kn1b4/p7/1P6/1NN5 w - - 0 1	29.688
2q5/2RNp1K1/b1Bk4/4N3/1nQ5/8/8/8 w - - 0 1	27.344
3K2Q1/4P3/1n1k4/8/4P3/8/2R5/q7 w - - 0 1	24.219
2q1b2k/5p1N/3N4/1P6/8/6R1/8/3K4 w - - 0 1	24.219
8/3P1k2/q2PpNRp/3PQ3/7K/5p2/8/8 w - - 0 1	28.125
8/8/7n/8/kP6/2K5/8/5n1R w - - 0 1	25.781
Nb6/1k1P4/nP1R4/1K6/8/8/8/8 w - - 0 1	21.875
3qk3/2rN1pP1/2RR1p2/Q7/5K1b/8/8/8 w - - 0 1	25.781
Qn6/6p1/8/8/1n6/8/1B1kP3/1K2b3 w - - 0 1	30.469
8/5P1k/K3N3/8/3B3r/6R1/6r1/8 w - - 0 1	26.562
1r1k1K2/P7/n6R/8/8/3b3B/4R3/8 w - - 0 1	24.219
8/8/8/1nBK4/8/3n4/7Q/5k2 w - - 0 1	21.094
3R4/4r3/4p3/8/8/6K1/8/3B1k2 w - - 0 1	15.625
7R/8/k1N1B3/2B5/8/2n5/5nK1/2r1b3 w - - 0 1	22.656
4r1k1/4b3/6PQ/8/2bK4/8/8/8 w - - 0 1	26.562
8/rpP2kP1/p5p1/5P2/7P/1bp4n/4Q3/5K2 w - - 0 1	30.469
8/5K2/7k/4R2B/4N3/5p2/pp5p/8 w - - 0 1	33.594
1k1N4/1P6/K7/8/5R2/8/8/8 w - - 0 1	21.875
6b1/5N1k/7b/6P1/3Q4/3n4/8/5K2 w - - 0 1	20.312
8/8/2p5/7R/r2p2N1/3k1K2/8/2R5 w - - 0 1	20.312
4Q3/8/3r4/8/8/6B1/7n/1r3k1K w - - 0 1	23.438
8/1R6/8/8/8/8/5r2/1Q1K1kb1 w - - 0 1	14.844
8/8/2Q5/2K2R1b/6Bk/8/6p1/6n1 w - - 0 1	19.531
8/1Pp4K/3b1N2/4n3/rk6/3npB2/1P6/2N5 w - - 0 1	32.812
8/8/2Q1K3/1N6/b7/1k6/2p5/8 w - - 0 1	27.344
7k/7q/3K3p/R7/8/8/8/5Q2 w - - 0 1	18.75
8/3Bk1b1/8/2K5/8/4BQ2/8/8 w - - 0 1	18.75
7N/5Prr/7k/5R2/8/2K5/8/8 w - - 0 1	17.969
8/p1Pp2P1/2n1kp2/2K5/Q1N5/7b/6p1/8 w - - 0 1	27.344
8/PK2Qr2/8/kpN5/8/2p5/8/8 w - - 0 1	26.562
2q5/3P4/3b1p2/3k4/8/2R2K2/8/7Q w - - 0 1	22.656

8/8/8/8/1nN5/4R2K/2p5/1qkN4 w - - 0 1	25
2rb4/5P2/4k1K1/8/8/8/8/3Q4 w - - 0 1	19.531
2r5/1P6/2b3Q1/K2B4/5B2/5p2/2p4p/7k w - - 0 1	21.094
8/8/b4R2/8/B7/8/k1K5/8 w - - 0 1	22.656
2B1n3/8/8/8/8/3NpKPb/4N1P1/5k2 w - - 0 1	23.438
5K2/4p3/1R6/8/6R1/k2p4/4P3/8 w - - 0 1	21.875
8/8/Kp6/1N6/k3q3/bp6/1nR5/4Q3 w - - 0 1	21.875
k7/2rN4/3P4/N7/7K/8/1pp5/2R5 w - - 0 1	25
1rn5/P2R4/1k6/q1R5/2P5/2P4K/8/8 w - - 0 1	25
2b2K2/5N1k/8/Q4R2/4n3/4q3/8/8 w - - 0 1	23.438
5k2/3P1r1r/8/6N1/8/4K3/8/8 w - - 0 1	12.5
3k4/N6N/p2PP3/4K3/5n2/8/8/8 w - - 0 1	19.531
3Q3n/3p2N1/3N4/1K1pk3/8/8/8/8 w - - 0 1	17.969
8/1N3k2/6p1/1Q1P1p1p/8/8/3B2K1/8 w - - 0 1	21.875
2R5/8/8/kbB5/Pp6/8/1Qn5/7K w - - 0 1	25.781
4q3/1K2B3/8/1p2R3/k4PR1/pp1N4/8/8 w - - 0 1	26.562
8/4r3/4k3/3pq3/8/8/6K1/1QQ5 w - - 0 1	23.438
8/8/4nK2/1R1Q4/5k2/5pq1/8/8 w - - 0 1	17.188
8/8/8/8/8/5b2/1Q2p2K/2bkN3 w - - 0 1	19.531
K7/8/1p6/8/7p/4bp1k/8/5NQ1 w - - 0 1	21.094
6Qn/3k1p2/8/N2B4/4p3/8/3K4/8 w - - 0 1	25
8/1B4b1/5Nb1/3pBk2/2Q5/6rN/5r2/2K5 w - - 0 1	28.906
8/1p6/2p5/P7/kBK5/2b3R1/8/8 w - - 0 1	24.219
3k1q2/4n3/2P5/4KN2/8/8/B1R5/8 w - - 0 1	22.656
6B1/5K2/1Bpp4/3k4/2p2b2/8/4P3/8 w - - 0 1	24.219
8/K7/8/6R1/8/5n1r/3B2bk w - - 0 1	25
1Q2R3/1r1k4/5p2/r7/3B4/8/4K3/7q w - - 0 1	22.656
8/8/3N4/8/1K1QN3/8/kP6/b2r4 w - - 0 1	24.219
3K4/r7/B7/N1Bk4/N7/2p1R3/b7/8 w - - 0 1	25.781
8/2p1B3/p5b1/k7/8/2K5/8/1R6 w - - 0 1	19.531
8/8/7r/8/3r4/8/8/1Q3K1k w - - 0 1	16.406
7k/K4Q1p/3b4/7R/4b3/8/8/8 w - - 0 1	18.75
4R3/2b5/8/8/8/2Q4K/kn6/8 w - - 0 1	20.312
2bb2K1/4PP1Q/2BkN3/qn6/3P4/8/4n3/8 w - - 0 1	29.688
r3r3/k7/8/1R2N3/1K6/8/1p4R1/8 w - - 0 1	30.469
5R1n/6P1/5K2/6p1/4pN2/4p1k1/5rP1/4B3 w - - 0 1	28.906

```
8/3p4/3p4/4k3/2rpN1K1/8/5RB1/1Q6 w - - 0 1          27.344
3K1Q1n/8/4B3/2PpkN2/8/3qpp1n/4N3/8 w - - 0 1        32.812
8/8/2K5/8/2kp4/1p6/1Q2R3/8 w - - 0 1                27.344
8/8/8/2n5/3B4/1B4p1/1p6/2k1KnQ1 w - - 0 1           16.406
8/8/r7/2Q1K3/k2r3R/2pN4/8/8 w - - 0 1               21.875
2R1r3/8/8/4Rr2/8/b4NK1/8/7k w - - 0 1               22.656
k1B1b3/1R1P4/1n6/P7/8/8/8/7K w - - 0 1              17.969
R3Q3/7r/1p5b/8/1K6/3N4/3n4/1k6 w - - 0 1            19.531
8/6P1/3rpp2/3nNPk1/5bbr/3K4/8/8 w - - 0 1           30.469
3k4/3pr2R/8/3pr3/8/8/1BR5/KQ1b4 w - - 0 1           31.25
4R3/P1k5/1bPr4/8/8/N7/2K5/8 w - - 0 1               27.344
8/8/8/3K4/5p1p/7B/Q3N3/4n2k w - - 0 1               25
7r/5Pn1/5NBk/4KRpp/8/8/8/8 w - - 0 1                28.125
8/8/4q3/p3p3/2p5/R7/3R4/1K3k2 w - - 0 1             25.781
3k4/3B4/2p5/3QK3/n7/2R5/3n4/8 w - - 0 1             20.312
K6k/6n1/7b/5n2/2Q5/7R/2B5/8 w - - 0 1               25
4rb1q/4k3/2R3pN/6N1/3p1p2/8/8/5KQ1 w - - 0 1        26.562
4R3/5kn1/6p1/5pp1/7Q/3R4/8/6KR w - - 0 1            24.219
3K4/rk5q/1P6/8/R7/8/B7/6B1 w - - 0 1                25.781
B7/8/2nn4/4b3/8/1k1K1Q2/1pN5/8 w - - 0 1            26.562
8/1R6/8/8/2K5/1r6/8/1k6 w - - 0 1                   17.969
1nN5/pk6/8/1N1KN3/8/8/8/8 w - - 0 1                 14.844
8/8/2p1Q3/5K2/4r3/8/4k3/7R w - - 0 1                20.312
1k1n4/4P3/8/1K6/8/8/8/8 w - - 0 1                   15.625
R7/4k3/4p3/5p1K/3B4/1n1Q4/7b/8 w - - 0 1            17.969
n1r5/1P6/b2N1K2/P1k5/1N6/3R4/8/8 w - - 0 1          25
1B1q4/1kP5/1r2B2b/5n1Q/2R3K1/4p3/8/8 w - - 0 1      32.031
5r2/1pnnK3/2p5/8/5N2/Np4Q1/3k4/6q1 w - - 0 1        32.812
B7/8/6rR/1k6/8/Q2K4/8/8 w - - 0 1                   25.781
5R2/6k1/4K3/8/4B2R/8/5p1n/1b6 w - - 0 1             21.875
8/8/8/8/N7/8/Q2p2K1/2k5 w - - 0 1                   20.312
8/6BK/8/6Np/5Nrk/1q4bP/6P1/8 w - - 0 1              22.656
8/6P1/7k/5B2/K5R1/8/8/7q w - - 0 1                  21.875
4k3/3r4/4P1b1/8/5R2/K7/4Q3/8 w - - 0 1              20.312
8/4P3/1b6/p5n1/8/1k1K3Q/8/2B5 w - - 0 1             23.438
8/8/8/8/6B1/8/5bnQ/5k1K w - - 0 1                   21.875
```

```
4R3/kpP5/nq2R3/8/8/7K/8/8 w - - 0 1                     21.875
2qkB1R1/1P2bb2/4nN2/1N6/8/4K3/8/8 w - - 0 1             22.656
qk6/pnN1P3/8/3R4/8/5K2/8/8 w - - 0 1                    25
8/3p4/r1p1n3/N1p5/2N5/3pK3/1B6/3kN3 w - - 0 1           31.25
8/K2N4/8/8/3k4/N5B1/4B1B1/8 w - - 0 1                   27.344
3b4/8/8/8/2K1k3/5RB1/4n1pQ/8 w - - 0 1                  15.625
q2b2R1/1Bk5/1NPp4/2P5/8/8/8/3K4 w - - 0 1               25
6R1/6N1/4Qq2/4pb2/2K1R3/6k1/5n1p/8 w - - 0 1            29.688
3K4/8/6Qn/8/k7/1nP5/bp6/8 w - - 0 1                     29.688
2B5/5K2/1bp2B2/1b1k1N2/4n3/8/8/8 w - - 0 1              26.562
8/5p2/7Q/6B1/8/2n5/8/1r1k1K2 w - - 0 1                  22.656
3Q4/8/6K1/2N5/5N2/4b1k1/8/8 w - - 0 1                   20.312
2r1k3/1q1R1b2/4N3/2N5/8/8/K3B1Q1/8 w - - 0 1            21.875
5K2/8/B7/8/N7/2b2R2/2bk1B2/8 w - - 0 1                  28.125
2k3q1/K1NR1b2/8/2p1Q3/8/8/8/8 w - - 0 1                 25
8/8/8/2Q5/3Nkr2/8/1Pb2nK1/7N w - - 0 1                  24.219
6k1/7N/6P1/8/4R3/2p2K2/8/8 w - - 0 1                    21.094
3nk2b/2Pp4/8/5N2/8/6KR/8/5Q2 w - - 0 1                  23.438
8/7Q/3K4/1q6/R7/1kp5/3PN3/8 w - - 0 1                   26.562
3K4/1N6/8/8/7Q/1k6/np6/1N6 w - - 0 1                    20.312
kb6/8/K7/4p3/1N1p4/2n4B/8/8 w - - 0 1                   23.438
8/4PPkr/K5N1/6r1/8/8/8/8 w - - 0 1                      20.312
2R5/5K2/8/3k4/N4R1N/4r3/5q2/8 w - - 0 1                 21.094
qN2B2K/pkP5/8/3N4/8/8/8/8 w - - 0 1                     22.656
3R4/P3n3/8/6K1/3Bk3/5q2/8/3B4 w - - 0 1                 22.656
8/8/6k1/q7/8/8/5Q2/2KQ4 w - - 0 1                       17.969
8/1K6/7N/4k3/6R1/3PB3/1p6/8 w - - 0 1                   18.75
8/5Q2/4N3/1p6/8/1K2k3/1R2n3/8 w - - 0 1                 17.188
2B5/8/1Q6/1K6/6pp/7k/7B/8 w - - 0 1                     19.531
6b1/5k2/5N2/4Q3/3K4/4B3/8/8 w - - 0 1                   20.312
3k1K2/7B/1Pp5/2p2NN1/8/8/8/8 w - - 0 1                  21.875
2RN1BB1/2pkP3/p7/3K4/8/7q/8/8 w - - 0 1                 23.438
6K1/6n1/4Q3/8/2q5/7R/2p5/rkr5 w - - 0 1                 25
8/1B5K/3p4/4k3/8/3P1B2/5Q2 w - - 0 1                    25
8/3p3Q/8/8/4K3/8/p7/4B1k1 w - - 0 1                     17.969
4Bk2/8/3P4/8/8/3p4/8/4K1Q1 w - - 0 1                    14.062
```

```
3kB3/8/1p6/QN6/8/8/2K5/8 w - - 0 1                        15.625
2Q2B2/4N1pP/K3pkp1/6q1/8/8/8/8 w - - 0 1                  25
5KB1/8/3p4/4kp1N/8/4BR2/8/8 w - - 0 1                     25.781
3k1K2/P2N4/3B4/7B/n7/4n3/8/8 w - - 0 1                    14.844
5Q2/6B1/8/8/6qp/5Pk1/K4Npr/1R6 w - - 0 1                  27.344
3r4/2P5/K1kqB3/8/8/8/8/1R6 w - - 0 1                      25
QB4R1/5k2/3b4/4Pr2/8/8/2K5/8 w - - 0 1                    21.094
7K/4p3/nB5k/5R2/6B1/8/8/8 w - - 0 1                       21.094
2bK4/k2P4/1pR1N3/8/8/8/3Q3r/8 w - - 0 1                   22.656
8/6b1/5k2/6pQ/8/4RbK1/5B2/5R2 w - - 0 1                   28.125
1NK1k2n/1N6/3B2pP/8/2p5/8/8/8 w - - 0 1                   28.125
8/1N6/8/3k1P2/5K2/8/1Q6/n7 w - - 0 1                      20.312
8/B1k5/8/8/6K1/1B6/1Q6/8 w - - 0 1                        14.062
1Q4Kb/2n2r2/8/3Nk3/4p1Bp/8/Q7/8 w - - 0 1                 20.312
R7/1BN5/8/7k/8/1pB4K/1n6/8 w - - 0 1                      27.344
8/2QP4/8/5k2/8/b1q5/4K3/2B3R1 w - - 0 1                   20.312
5N2/1K2n3/7p/7k/6pr/8/4PB2/5Q2 w - - 0 1                  25.781
4N1b1/4kBB1/7K/4NP2/8/8/8/8 w - - 0 1                     23.438
7K/5B2/5p1k/6r1/8/6N1/4RP2/8 w - - 0 1                    19.531
6Q1/3P4/8/5r1k/7N/8/K4P2/8 w - - 0 1                      20.312
8/K7/8/k7/8/2PB4/2n3Q1/7b w - - 0 1                       21.875
3q4/2pQ4/1pN5/8/k2N4/b4K2/8/8 w - - 0 1                   25
3krn2/6P1/3N2q1/4P3/6QK/8/8/6B1 w - - 0 1                 27.344
1N6/8/1p6/2kP4/1pPp1B2/5K2/8/3R4 w - - 0 1                31.25
kN6/1pB2P2/8/8/N7/8/2K2p2/8 w - - 0 1                     25
kb6/8/2K5/6Q1/2p5/1b6/8/8 w - - 0 1                       16.406
1b6/1KP5/8/1k6/b7/2B5/8/8 w - - 0 1                       15.625
8/P1k5/8/4N3/3Q4/8/3K4/4N1r1 w - - 0 1                    17.969
8/8/8/Q3b3/6R1/4rB1k/8/7K w - - 0 1                       19.531
8/8/2N2R2/7b/1R1r4/3pk3/3n4/1Q2K3 w - - 0 1               24.219
K1k2r2/2r3P1/8/1P6/3q4/8/B7/8 w - - 0 1                   25.781
1K2b2b/3P2k1/5R1q/6P1/4B3/8/8/8 w - - 0 1                 24.219
8/8/rp6/1k6/p2K4/1pB5/3Q4/2bB4 w - - 0 1                  29.688
8/4PN1k/4b3/5p2/7b/8/7K/6Q1 w - - 0 1                     28.125
4Q3/8/3NPkp1/3p4/6B1/8/8/3K4 w - - 0 1                    22.656
b2B4/1P6/3k4/8/8/4N3/7K/8 w - - 0 1                       19.531
```

b2b4/1P1p4/1k6/8/4r3/Q4K2/8/8 w - - 0 1	13.281
8/4R2P/3b1k1B/4q2B/8/8/6K1/8 w - - 0 1	25
8/4Q3/7B/1b3p1q/8/8/k7/2K5 w - - 0 1	15.625
8/2K5/8/1N6/4Q3/1pp5/pkp5/4R3 w - - 0 1	20.312
N7/2p5/1p6/3K4/kB6/8/8/8 w - - 0 1	21.094
3n4/k3P3/r7/2P5/8/1Q3BK1/8/8 w - - 0 1	21.875
8/1K6/1N6/kN6/1nB2R2/8/4b3/8 w - - 0 1	25
8/8/8/7r/3pp3/3R4/B1K3R1/k7 w - - 0 1	25
k7/1rpN4/8/8/8/8/KQ6 w - - 0 1	19.531
5K2/5P2/5k2/4R3/2N5/8/8/8 w - - 0 1	17.188
1k4K1/4P3/n7/8/3p4/4QB2/8/8 w - - 0 1	18.75
2K1k3/5R2/8/1R6/2Pp4/4p3/8/3q4 w - - 0 1	17.969
3b4/K1kB4/6pN/8/8/3RR3/8/8 w - - 0 1	22.656
K7/8/8/1p5B/kp6/1r4Q1/8/8 w - - 0 1	23.438
5b2/3P2R1/6R1/5k2/6R1/8/5p2/7K w - - 0 1	23.438
8/2R5/2qk1r2/4R3/2Q5/7K/5B2/8 w - - 0 1	22.656
8/8/1Q6/5b2/3p4/1R3K2/n1B5/4k3 w - - 0 1	25
5K1k/6pp/b5P1/8/8/8/5B2/1B6 w - - 0 1	25
8/4N1k1/K7/8/5R2/6P1/2N5/8 w - - 0 1	17.188
8/5K2/4B3/8/1P2kPR1/1n1brN2/6q1/7Q w - - 0 1	25.781
8/8/8/1ppp4/3p4/2k5/K4QR1/2qR4 w - - 0 1	32.031
5kn1/3B2pP/4PBP1/8/2q5/8/8/6K1 w - - 0 1	31.25
1K6/p7/6R1/8/5k1N/4b2n/8/7Q w - - 0 1	25.781
8/1K6/4Q3/8/8/2B5/2n1q3/nkN5 w - - 0 1	25
8/k1B5/4B2Q/7K/8/8/2r5/8 w - - 0 1	17.188
k7/2n5/1PK5/8/8/8/8/8 w - - 0 1	13.281
8/8/8/K7/1N6/2p1k3/7Q/2R5 w - - 0 1	15.625
7K/8/1R6/3p2B1/8/8/6B1/k7 w - - 0 1	18.75
5B2/2K5/4q3/8/8/1Np5/1rk5/1br2Q2 w - - 0 1	25
8/8/5n2/8/1bN5/8/p7/k1K1B3 w - - 0 1	24.219
8/8/2k1nR2/3r1N2/1Q5K/3B4/8/8 w - - 0 1	18.75
8/rk6/1P4Q1/pB6/1PK5/8/8/8 w - - 0 1	22.656
8/8/4bQ2/2K5/4B3/8/8/3n2k1 w - - 0 1	21.875
3K4/p5Q1/1k1B2R1/b7/1P6/8/8/8 w - - 0 1	21.875
8/b5B1/8/3k4/2R2K2/6Q1/8/8 w - - 0 1	17.188
2k2K2/1r6/1PP5/4N3/8/8/8/n4B2 w - - 0 1	21.875

8/4Q3/4p3/8/2B5/7n/2N5/K2k4 w - - 0 1	21.094
6Q1/4K3/B7/1pk5/b2N1R2/8/8/8 w - - 0 1	21.094
8/3B4/R3qb2/3p4/4kp2/5N2/4K3/3N4 w - - 0 1	23.438
1B6/8/2K5/6R1/8/6Nk/5b1n/5bQ1 w - - 0 1	29.688
4K3/2k1N3/Pp2p3/1n2PQ2/3P4/5n1b/8/8 w - - 0 1	30.469
2R5/4p3/2p1kr2/2Q5/8/8/4K2R/8 w - - 0 1	26.562
8/3k1K2/7B/N7/4B2b/8/5p2/8 w - - 0 1	23.438
3k3N/2R2R2/2n5/8/b7/6K1/3B4/8 w - - 0 1	21.094
8/8/2R5/8/5R2/3KP3/3b4/4k3 w - - 0 1	17.188
Q7/8/2N1k1K1/8/4p3/7N/4N3/4q3 w - - 0 1	17.188
8/1PQ1b3/k7/3n4/8/q7/2N5/1K6 w - - 0 1	25
4K3/P1k5/8/N7/8/8/7R/4b3 w - - 0 1	19.531
Q7/8/8/8/1K6/8/1kBp2rN/8 w - - 0 1	17.969
7N/7k/3Q4/8/5K2/4B3/8/4q3 w - - 0 1	20.312
1N6/1R1N3n/2P5/k7/8/8/8/7K w - - 0 1	17.969
4n1N1/8/2K3N1/7k/3Q4/8/8/8 w - - 0 1	17.969
8/3n4/2N5/6R1/8/1R1pK3/3PP3/2kr4 w - - 0 1	22.656
7R/4P3/3N1k2/8/8/Q7/n2K4/8 w - - 0 1	24.219
6R1/5r1n/2Q2rPR/6k1/8/5P2/7K/8 w - - 0 1	24.219
8/8/8/3K4/8/1R2N3/1q3npk/Q3N1R1 w - - 0 1	28.906
4k3/6r1/N1P2p2/2B5/8/Q7/5K2/8 w - - 0 1	25.781
8/8/4Q3/8/8/2n5/2k5/K3Qn2 w - - 0 1	21.875
7K/8/8/5B2/1n6/5k2/2Q2N2/8 w - - 0 1	16.406
R7/5Q2/1Kp4B/8/b7/k3p3/8/8 w - - 0 1	21.875
2B1kB2/8/8/6K1/8/8/R7/8 w - - 0 1	20.312
4k3/3Nrp2/3nN3/4q3/4R3/2Q1K3/8/3R4 w - - 0 1	21.875
b4BQ1/6p1/B1P3K1/8/4P3/2k1p3/8/8 w - - 0 1	25.781
r2bk3/Q7/8/3B4/3R1q2/8/8/3K4 w - - 0 1	25.781
8/4N2p/4p3/3B4/p7/2B5/K7/3k1B2 w - - 0 1	21.094
4k3/8/5K2/8/8/5N2/6p1/7R w - - 0 1	21.875
k7/4pQ2/2R5/1N6/6q1/8/5K2/8 w - - 0 1	18.75
8/8/P3p3/K1k1P3/6B1/8/8/1Q4b1 w - - 0 1	21.094
2r1k3/3p1R2/2N5/3K2R1/8/8/8/3B4 w - - 0 1	25
8/r1n5/8/8/3Q4/2n1K3/2R5/1k6 w - - 0 1	23.438
8/2k5/2N1B3/8/1K2n3/1Q6/8/8 w - - 0 1	17.969
5k2/4p3/5N1K/8/8/8/4B3/1R6 w - - 0 1	18.75

FEN	Value
2k5/5P2/1Rp5/8/4p3/1p6/3K4/4Q3 w - - 0 1	21.875
8/8/R7/8/1K6/B7/B2p4/k7 w - - 0 1	19.531
8/8/8/8/N7/B7/4p2R/K3kb2 w - - 0 1	14.844
7Q/8/3pn3/4p3/2N3K1/1B6/N7/5k2 w - - 0 1	22.656
KR6/5n2/3p4/2k5/8/3Q2p1/4P3/8 w - - 0 1	23.438
7Q/8/4B3/4n3/8/1K1kqP1p/5B2/1N6 w - - 0 1	25.781
8/5K2/2kp4/2N5/N7/8/8/3Q4 w - - 0 1	25
5q1Q/2P1P3/K2k4/B3R3/8/8/8/5r2 w - - 0 1	21.094
8/1K6/N7/1k6/8/1pq3r1/Q3R3/2RB4 w - - 0 1	27.344
6B1/5N2/K1k2N2/B7/8/8/N7/8 w - - 0 1	21.875
R4K2/1pPr4/1b1kb3/Q7/8/8/4B3/8 w - - 0 1	24.219
8/8/2b5/2RN1k2/3n3B/7K/6B1/8 w - - 0 1	28.125
2K3B1/5n2/2nN4/3kp3/8/8/3BQ3/8 w - - 0 1	21.875
1Q6/8/Kb5R/8/8/8/6k1/1R2r2b w - - 0 1	26.562
2N1B3/7p/4k3/6Q1/8/2K2P2/4p3/8 w - - 0 1	25
2B5/2K5/Q1p5/8/7k/1R4p1/1p4r1/8 w - - 0 1	24.219
4K3/8/5R2/5P1k/1Q6/7q/8/4bN2 w - - 0 1	26.562
8/8/8/5N2/8/B7/3pp3/1B2k1K1 w - - 0 1	18.75
QK6/1NB1b3/B1k5/8/8/1n6/8/8 w - - 0 1	23.438
8/K2Q4/8/1N6/8/8/3pk2B/2Rb4 w - - 0 1	25
8/4B3/8/2p1k3/4P3/4K3/5R2/8 w - - 0 1	21.875
6k1/8/4KR1P/8/R5r1/8/8/8 w - - 0 1	18.75
4Q3/4b3/5k2/8/5K2/5N2/8/8 w - - 0 1	14.844
7k/6Nq/6b1/7R/8/1B6/7Q/5K2 w - - 0 1	20.312
8/4K3/5R2/6pk/7r/6r1/Q7/q7 w - - 0 1	22.656
6n1/6Pk/4NrNr/4KP2/8/8/2Q3q1/7R w - - 0 1	28.906
3KB3/3N1N2/8/5k2/2R5/8/8/8 w - - 0 1	25.781
8/1R6/8/2bk3K/7Q/8/8/B7 w - - 0 1	18.75
R4R2/1k6/2p5/8/3K4/2p5/8/8 w - - 0 1	16.406
3k4/4p3/2KP4/8/1B6/8/8/8 w - - 0 1	14.844
4K3/3BN3/4nR2/3P1p2/3Pk1p1/3bPN2/4rPq1/8 w - - 0 1	30.469
K7/p2p3P/r1p5/7k/p6p/8/8/4R3 w - - 0 1	38.281
3Q4/p2B4/K1p5/2k1Pn2/5P2/4pr2/N7/8 w - - 0 1	23.438
3Q4/1p2K3/2kP4/6N1/4p3/4NP2/8/8 w - - 0 1	22.656
3Bk2r/5r1N/1N4B1/8/4b3/1K2Q3/8/8 w - - 0 1	22.656
8/8/3p2K1/2bkN3/4p1B1/2P3r1/6NQ/8 w - - 0 1	28.125

```
k7/6N1/2P5/8/4Kp2/8/2p5/B6Q w - - 0 1                      27.344
Bb2r3/B2K4/8/8/4p1N1/8/2R5/7k w - - 0 1                    17.188
Q2q4/8/8/2N5/8/8/2Kn1N2/4k3 w - - 0 1                      20.312
1Q6/8/8/5N2/3K2k1/8/1p4P1/8 w - - 0 1                      20.312
5R2/2NP1q2/2k1r3/2B1r3/8/7Q/8/K2R4 w - - 0 1               26.562
3K4/n6p/8/1Q6/1Np3pk/4N3/8/R7 w - - 0 1                    30.469
7R/5k2/n1K3R1/7P/2p2p2/6N1/8/8 w - - 0 1                   26.562
8/8/4B2p/4B2k/4K2p/8/8/8 w - - 0 1                         21.094
Q3R3/8/8/qp6/3k4/8/1N3K2/6B1 w - - 0 1                     21.875
K7/8/k1p5/r7/8/2N5/8/3Q4 w - - 0 1                         17.188
3K4/8/8/6p1/4NPrk/5P1r/4P3/5Q2 w - - 0 1                   25
4Q3/8/8/2N5/3k1n2/6N1/2K5/2n5 w - - 0 1                    24.219
1n6/k1N5/P7/2RBN3/bp5K/2b5/5pQ1/8 w - - 0 1                28.906
8/P4N2/8/1k1PN3/8/1K6/4p3/8 w - - 0 1                      23.438
1bk5/3N4/2K5/8/5NB1/8/8/8 w - - 0 1                        20.312
7K/5p2/8/B5k1/5p2/7Q/8/7b w - - 0 1                        17.969
8/K3B3/4N1r1/3kp3/4n3/3PQ3/8/4N3 w - - 0 1                 26.562
8/8/8/3N2RK/2pkp2p/2p5/3rR3/2B2B2 w - - 0 1                29.688
8/2N1Np2/4n3/4k3/1Q2b3/2N1P3/1K2n3/8 w - - 0 1             28.906
k1K1Q3/8/2N5/8/8/8/2P5/4r3 w - - 0 1                       26.562
6Q1/4B3/6p1/3K4/8/4k3/8/2b2R2 w - - 0 1                    20.312
8/7b/8/5N2/kN6/1p6/1p6/1K3Q2 w - - 0 1                     21.094
8/3N4/6R1/3k3K/4r3/4p3/2pN4/3Q1B2 w - - 0 1                25.781
5KB1/8/7Q/8/8/k1N2p2/p7/8 w - - 0 1                        26.562
3Bn2K/8/2N5/8/2rp4/5R2/2Prk3/5R2 w - - 0 1                 25.781
8/3pK3/4n3/2rk4/8/Q2B4/7R/8 w - - 0 1                      29.688
8/4n3/8/8/K2NB3/5R2/3p4/k7 w - - 0 1                       21.094
1Kb3R1/4N3/8/1p2k1B1/3b4/Q2P4/2p1N3/8 w - - 0 1            25
8/8/k7/1NBK4/n2B4/2B5/1p6/8 w - - 0 1                      26.562
b7/3K4/2R5/8/1k6/8/1P6/7Q w - - 0 1                        19.531
B7/8/7n/1Q1K4/8/8/7B/3R1bnk w - - 0 1                      18.75
5R2/8/8/2R5/2P1k2K/1br1b3/Q4P2/8 w - - 0 1                 29.688
2rB4/5R2/3k4/2nP1K2/2B5/8/3b4/5Q2 w - - 0 1                26.562
5nQ1/2K2P2/8/8/3p1N2/4k3/6R1/8 w - - 0 1                   25.781
1N6/1k1B4/1P6/BK6/8/4n3/8/8 w - - 0 1                      21.094
3k3b/KPN5/1n6/8/2P5/5Q2/8/8 w - - 0 1                      18.75
```

8/8/3BK3/8/2NkN3/3p4/8/3B4 w - - 0 1	21.094
8/8/8/8/3B1K2/1kppn3/8/Rq1R1Q2 w - - 0 1	18.75
4r1r1/3RnN2/2b1k1qQ/6B1/8/8/8/KB6 w - - 0 1	29.688
8/3p4/8/3B4/1P5R/k3N3/8/1K2n3 w - - 0 1	26.562
5nQ1/K7/N1k1n3/8/2P1N3/8/8/6r1 w - - 0 1	26.562
8/8/1p6/2k5/1p1N1K2/2rP4/5Q2/8 w - - 0 1	26.562
8/8/3RN3/8/k7/2B2n2/1K1p4/8 w - - 0 1	21.094
nk6/pP2N3/B7/2rn4/8/3R4/1B1Q2K1/8 w - - 0 1	25
7k/8/4NP2/7P/8/2K5/8/8 w - - 0 1	26.562
4B3/8/2b5/K6p/7k/Q3R3/8/8 w - - 0 1	16.406
8/2p5/1kN5/8/2Q1K3/8/2p5/3b2R1 w - - 0 1	21.094
8/8/5K2/1n1BRb2/5kNB/2Rq2p1/6p1/8 w - - 0 1	31.25
5N2/4pBkp/7N/4p3/4p1n1/2Rp1P2/8/1b4K1 w - - 0 1	30.469
6r1/8/K5p1/3B4/1p6/k7/5B1R/8 w - - 0 1	34.375
8/P1b5/1R5n/2p4K/2k5/3p1B2/5Q2/2n5 w - - 0 1	27.344
8/7Q/4pr1R/3pk3/8/2K5/8/4B3 w - - 0 1	27.344
8/6N1/7K/4k3/8/4N3/3Bn1B1/4Q3 w - - 0 1	17.188
8/8/8/2N5/5k2/8/2KbB1Q1/8 w - - 0 1	14.844
n1r5/kbRP4/1Np5/2K5/1N6/8/8/8 w - - 0 1	22.656
8/8/1N1b4/6QB/8/1k6/6K1/8 w - - 0 1	21.875
8/4kn2/3pBR2/8/Q7/4P3/8/7K w - - 0 1	19.531
8/3B4/4p3/8/2kB4/8/8/1b1QK3 w - - 0 1	21.094
8/2pN4/2k5/Pp6/3K4/5R2/n7/Q7 w - - 0 1	20.312
8/8/8/1KNk4/8/5P2/R7/8 w - - 0 1	14.844
8/8/b1k5/5B2/5B2/Q7/8/K7 w - - 0 1	17.188
8/8/2N5/2k2B2/8/4N1K1/5Q2 w - - 0 1	13.281
8/3Q4/5k2/8/1B2P3/6b1/4K3/8 w - - 0 1	16.406
2r5/1P3k2/8/6Q1/8/6K1/8/8 w - - 0 1	14.844
5K2/1B5P/8/7B/P1k1N3/P2r4/P4P2/8 w - - 0 1	22.656
4k3/3rp3/R3PB2/3n4/2K2Q2/8/7q/3Q4 w - - 0 1	32.031
8/8/3B3b/5Knk/8/6P1/8/8 w - - 0 1	26.562
6b1/8/4p3/b7/1R4K1/7Q/8/4k3 w - - 0 1	20.312
4K3/5p2/4B1p1/4k3/3R4/4b3/1N6/7Q w - - 0 1	22.656
1K6/1P6/B7/8/p7/2n2p2/4Q3/k7 w - - 0 1	26.562
2N5/4N1k1/K5p1/8/8/8/1pp5/7Q w - - 0 1	22.656
5B2/8/7P/8/8/2p5/1p3K2/R4b1k w - - 0 1	19.531

```
6B1/1N6/2Q5/7K/5p2/4R2p/2r2r2/2k1B3 w - - 0 1           27.344
6r1/5K2/1N4P1/2p1NkN1/R7/2p3P1/8/8 w - - 0 1            32.031
8/4p3/4k3/5b2/B4P1N/1K6/8/Q7 w - - 0 1                  25
8/6k1/8/3n4/6N1/8/8/R1K1Q3 w - - 0 1                    19.531
8/8/5B1Q/8/k4K2/r1p5/2PR4/8 w - - 0 1                   21.875
8/8/8/r2BpRP1/8/2B2KPk/1R6/5b2 w - - 0 1                27.344
1N3R2/4p3/ppp1k3/8/5R2/8/5K1N/8 w - - 0 1               32.812
k2K4/8/PP1P4/8/n7/8/8/8 w - - 0 1                       20.312
kNK5/8/8/8/3p1B2/8/8/8 w - - 0 1                        14.062
6K1/1Q6/8/5n2/2k5/1p6/N1np4/2Q1b3 w - - 0 1             23.438
2k5/3p4/5Q2/4P3/8/4K3/8/8 w - - 0 1                     23.438
1R6/8/3k1K2/6N1/p1P4p/2p5/2R5/8 w - - 0 1               19.531
8/1Rq2P1k/4B3/8/7K/8/8/8 w - - 0 1                      21.094
8/5N1k/2p3N1/4K3/8/8/8/6N1 w - - 0 1                    13.281
k7/8/P7/Kp6/5N2/5R2/7p/8 w - - 0 1                      20.312
8/N7/3N2p1/k4b1n/B7/BB3K2/2pb4/8 w - - 0 1              25
3B2b1/1k1K1R2/1Npb4/8/1Nb5/1B2p3/5R2/1R6 w - - 0 1      35.156
k7/4N3/1n1p4/1K6/8/3Rp2r/6pp/6Q1 w - - 0 1              31.25
5NK1/R6p/4P1pk/8/5NP1/8/3pq3/8 w - - 0 1                34.375
8/8/5Q2/1q6/6PK/8/p3PBR1/1k6 w - - 0 1                  25.781
bNBK4/k2nBN2/p4P2/1R1N4/7b/p7/8/8 w - - 0 1             28.906
5RK1/3k4/8/8/8/4n3/2R3R1/1n6 w - - 0 1                  30.469
8/8/5k1n/1K3p2/8/1p4p1/1p2Q3/1Q6 w - - 0 1              22.656
2k3q1/1N6/8/8/1K1Q4/8/8/5Q2 w - - 0 1                   23.438
1k6/3p2P1/2P5/2K5/8/3B3r/8/8 w - - 0 1                  20.312
8/P6K/8/8/4R3/3n4/8/5N1k w - - 0 1                      17.969
8/6K1/8/p4B2/k7/2P5/4Q3/1n2n3 w - - 0 1                 21.875
8/8/7K/8/8/1k1N4/1p6/1R2R3 w - - 0 1                    17.188
6k1/2N5/6P1/7N/5K2/8/6b1/8 w - - 0 1                    18.75
5R2/6k1/r1p5/8/b7/3QK3/8/n7 w - - 0 1                   21.875
2K4R/8/1p2N3/3pn3/5p2/2Q2n2/8/5k2 w - - 0 1             28.125
8/1q6/1Q6/2rn4/5P2/7P/3B1K1k/1R6 w - - 0 1              24.219
3K2N1/8/6nB/3pk3/2p2p2/1R3Q2/8/8 w - - 0 1              26.562
8/8/1p1k1K2/3B2r1/2RN3Q/7R/1b6/8 w - - 0 1              26.562
1b3k1K/2P5/7R/8/8/8/8/8 w - - 0 1                       23.438
2Nk1nR1/6n1/8/8/8/8/8/4KQ2 w - - 0 1                    16.406
```

```
8/5P2/4N1p1/8/5K1k/8/8/8 w - - 0 1                    18.75
2n5/2B4K/2R5/8/7k/7B/4p2P/8 w - - 0 1                 17.188
8/4N3/2R5/1B6/1k4p1/7p/5BpK/1N6 w - - 0 1             20.312
8/B7/8/2b4r/1N2kP1n/1K1n2PQ/2R2pp1/3nN3 w - - 0 1     30.469
3B4/8/k7/8/8/2Q2K2/3q4/8 w - - 0 1                    32.812
1R4Bk/1K2B3/6q1/8/6N1/4B3/6n1/8 w - - 0 1             21.875
8/3R2B1/8/8/8/p4p2/5k1K/N7 w - - 0 1                  25
q7/3K4/8/3BR3/3nR3/6N1/5k2/8 w - - 0 1                17.969
8/5N2/8/2QK2p1/6PN/6pk/6p1/8 w - - 0 1                21.875
5r2/6Q1/8/7k/4K3/5P1p/8/3N4 w - - 0 1                 22.656
8/8/BQ6/4k3/p7/1P6/4P2K/8 w - - 0 1                   21.875
8/8/7R/K2Nr1N1/5R2/3kpN2/8/8 w - - 0 1                22.656
1r6/2P5/5k2/8/2R5/n4P2/1P4KR/r1b5 w - - 0 1           28.906
Nk6/6R1/P3N3/1P2b3/2K2P2/2p5/6p1/1r6 w - - 0 1        28.906
8/2p5/6pN/8/8/1K6/2R5/2N1k3 w - - 0 1                 29.688
8/8/8/2Q1qq2/1B6/2P2k1B/1R5P/3N1Kb1 w - - 0 1         29.688
```

Disliked Database

```
8/1Kp5/8/8/N1Q5/q2B4/3p3N/3k4 w - - 0 1               0
4k3/B6K/3q4/5R2/8/8/Q4p2/8 w - - 0 1                  25
3b1kbr/1K6/4R3/3Q3r/8/8/8/8 w - - 0 1                 23.438
6Q1/8/5P2/2p4K/1b6/2N5/7k/1r6 w - - 0 1               20.312
6bk/8/3B2K1/R1P5/3b4/P4B2/6P1/8 w - - 0 1             23.438
8/q7/3R4/5Q2/4K3/Bk6/8/8 w - - 0 1                    20.312
2K1k3/7P/8/1n2b3/8/5Q2/8/8 w - - 0 1                  18.75
6bQ/4K3/1k6/8/8/8/P7/8 w - - 0 1                      17.188
5n2/7k/7N/8/6K1/8/Q3p3/5b2 w - - 0 1                  16.406
8/8/8/2K5/8/2Q3n1/b7/1k5B w - - 0 1                   17.969
3n1K2/8/7N/2Bkp1p1/5p2/7B/4Q3/8 w - - 0 1             22.656
6R1/1R3b1q/8/6b1/8/2Q5/8/4K2k w - - 0 1               25.781
8/7B/8/2r5/k7/7p/4R3/K6R w - - 0 1                    18.75
8/P5q1/8/3k1Bp1/1B1r4/n7/6K1/Q7 w - - 0 1             24.219
7k/2B5/4K3/8/8/3n4/4R3/8 w - - 0 1                    23.438
```

2B2qk1/8/4n1K1/8/8/8/7B/8 w - - 0 1	14.844
8/p3b3/6R1/3r4/1pK5/1B6/1R6/7k w - - 0 1	21.094
8/4P3/8/1P6/8/8/4R3/K5kr w - - 0 1	18.75
8/8/8/3K4/8/8/kBN5/1n1Q4 w - - 0 1	18.75
8/8/1k3K1b/3RpQ2/6b1/8/2Br4/5R2 w - - 0 1	20.312
k1N5/1b6/8/4p3/8/1B6/2QK4/8 w - - 0 1	18.75
8/7p/5p2/5k2/8/4QP2/6K1/8 w - - 0 1	20.312
8/6P1/8/8/p7/K7/Bp6/7k w - - 0 1	18.75
8/8/5Q2/8/2K5/6b1/8/4k3 w - - 0 1	15.625
2K5/8/k7/4B3/B7/3N4/3N2p1/8 w - - 0 1	17.188
2R2b2/8/8/8/3p3k/1K6/3Q4/5b2 w - - 0 1	17.188
3B4/1K6/1p6/1kN5/br6/3P4/8/5Q2 w - - 0 1	22.656
4R3/K7/N7/1k6/8/8/8/8 w - - 0 1	17.188
8/8/8/5B2/8/3K4/6k1/4BN2 w - - 0 1	14.062
1R6/7K/8/8/2p5/2p3R1/8/4k3 w - - 0 1	14.844
6K1/2N5/8/5R2/k7/8/5p2/5N2 w - - 0 1	18.75
8/8/1Q2p3/2n5/8/4K3/6k1/8 w - - 0 1	17.188
8/8/3qpB2/7R/4r3/3Br1k1/K7/2Q5 w - - 0 1	17.969
8/8/1n1R4/8/8/2K5/8/k7 w - - 0 1	19.531
5rk1/7p/6n1/6q1/3B4/4Q3/3K4/1B6 w - - 0 1	20.312
8/2P4r/4k1r1/8/3Q4/6n1/6K1 w - - 0 1	20.312
7n/5b2/6B1/8/5k1K/8/6Q1 w - - 0 1	15.625
8/3r2k1/4R3/8/8/6q1/2R5/1K3Q2 w - - 0 1	20.312
8/4k3/1R1n2K1/8/5N2/1p6/5q2/2R5 w - - 0 1	23.438
1Q2K3/8/6p1/8/8/4R3/q4kn1/7B w - - 0 1	20.312
4K3/8/8/5Q2/5N1r/8/8/3Bk3 w - - 0 1	18.75
4k3/8/8/3K3R/5Bp1/8/8/8 w - - 0 1	12.5
3r1Q2/8/3R4/8/5K2/8/8/7k w - - 0 1	13.281
b7/8/1Q6/8/8/1K4R1/5p2/2k5 w - - 0 1	17.188
8/4B3/8/1p3r2/8/K4p2/N2N4/k1n2r2 w - - 0 1	22.656
8/7p/3RB3/8/4K2k/8/8/8 w - - 0 1	23.438
3b4/4R1B1/8/8/6B1/K7/8/1k6 w - - 0 1	17.188
8/8/8/3p3r/2b1Q3/4K3/8/2kNR3 w - - 0 1	21.875
8/7p/8/1b1B4/2RP4/7k/4RK2/8 w - - 0 1	20.312
8/6P1/8/7n/K6k/4b3/6R1/8 w - - 0 1	21.875
5b2/1Q5K/4B2N/8/5k2/r2P4/3n1N2/6B1 w - - 0 1	26.562

5Q2/8/7p/6k1/4r3/5BB1/b7/3K4 w - - 0 1	25
2R2KN1/7k/8/8/8/4rn2/2R5/8 w - - 0 1	18.75
N1b5/rkP5/2p5/7r/2Q5/8/4K3/6R1 w - - 0 1	24.219
7k/6r1/8/6P1/4R3/5B2/p2K4/6B1 w - - 0 1	25.781
1r6/p7/k2K4/8/3R2Q1/2b5/r7/1R6 w - - 0 1	24.219
6R1/8/8/8/2K5/8/1b6/k7 w - - 0 1	20.312
5Q2/2B4n/8/2K5/4p3/k7/8/8 w - - 0 1	15.625
5n2/8/1Q6/8/2B5/7k/8/4K3 w - - 0 1	14.844
8/k7/2p5/8/4P3/2PN4/1KP5/3Q4 w - - 0 1	20.312
3R4/8/3p1K2/8/1p6/Qr3R2/ppP3p1/3kB3 w - - 0 1	25
6k1/1P2B3/7R/1q5B/8/4b3/2p5/K2R4 w - - 0 1	31.25
8/5B2/N7/1k6/1N6/K7/5p2/B7 w - - 0 1	21.875
1b6/1p2K3/b7/4Q3/4B3/8/kP6/8 w - - 0 1	21.094
8/8/3q4/K7/3p4/R4N2/2kn1p2/Q7 w - - 0 1	26.562
K6N/Q7/B6k/8/8/8/8/5n2 w - - 0 1	23.438
4B3/6kr/4P3/4R3/K7/8/1B6/8 w - - 0 1	20.312
1b5k/8/8/7K/8/8/b7/2Q5 w - - 0 1	18.75
2rN1kq1/8/5K2/8/3NRb2/6Q1/2r5/8 w - - 0 1	23.438
q7/8/8/2K2Q2/N7/1k6/8/8 w - - 0 1	23.438
8/3B4/5R2/8/2K5/8/3k4/8 w - - 0 1	14.062
8/8/8/5BB1/8/8/5k1K/6N1 w - - 0 1	14.062
2b3Q1/7K/R7/5n2/1R6/4B2k/5r2/8 w - - 0 1	17.188
8/8/8/1K3Q2/2B5/5r2/1B4k1/8 w - - 0 1	21.094
8/8/n4Q2/5q2/3P4/R7/2b5/1knR3K w - - 0 1	22.656
1Nk3B1/1p6/5K2/8/8/8/8/7Q w - - 0 1	20.312
q7/2K5/R7/1k3N2/N7/2B5/8/8 w - - 0 1	20.312
k7/8/7p/8/5B2/p1K5/7p/4Q3 w - - 0 1	17.188
8/P7/8/3B3p/8/8/2K1k3/8 w - - 0 1	18.75
8/KQ6/6N1/1R6/1R5n/2k3rb/1N6/8 w - - 0 1	21.094
8/8/B7/2Q5/8/3n4/1n6/1K1k4 w - - 0 1	22.656
1RN5/5p2/5k2/8/1q1PQ3/6K1/8/8 w - - 0 1	21.875
3q4/8/5N2/2R5/Rn1k4/K5bQ/3P4/8 w - - 0 1	18.75
8/2P1K3/pN6/k7/8/B7/7p/8 w - - 0 1	24.219
1b5N/7p/7k/R7/7K/8/8/8 w - - 0 1	17.969
4R3/8/5b2/8/2K5/8/8/k7 w - - 0 1	15.625
8/2K5/k1p5/8/B7/8/8/6B1 w - - 0 1	14.062

2k5/8/3P4/3K4/8/4R3/N2p4/8 w - - 0 1	17.188
3k4/8/3N1K2/8/6R1/8/8/8 w - - 0 1	13.281
4R3/8/8/5p2/5k2/7B/6K1/8 w - - 0 1	14.062
8/5nP1/8/8/5rk1/8/8/1Q5K w - - 0 1	14.844
8/6Q1/K7/1N6/8/3Pr3/Bnk2p2/5q2 w - - 0 1	22.656
2k5/Pr6/3K4/8/8/8/8/8 w - - 0 1	21.875
5K2/2Q5/8/b6N/1N6/8/4Bk2/8 w - - 0 1	17.188
8/1r6/6Q1/8/2B5/k2K4/6n1/8 w - - 0 1	20.312
5b2/8/8/4Nk2/8/5K2/3N2Q1/8 w - - 0 1	16.406
8/5p2/5RR1/5p2/2R3P1/3k3n/5B2/3K4 w - - 0 1	22.656
8/8/2q1N3/2p5/5Q1K/1k2B3/R7/8 w - - 0 1	28.125
6b1/7P/3P4/8/K7/4k3/8/8 w - - 0 1	17.969
2R5/1k1N4/q7/4B3/4K3/8/p7/Q7 w - - 0 1	20.312
8/2R5/k7/2PK4/5pp1/1P6/8 w - - 0 1	23.438
2RQ4/8/2K4b/8/4k1N1/3r1R2/3P1n2/8 w - - 0 1	21.875
4b3/N7/7n/3K4/k7/4Qp2/8/8 w - - 0 1	21.875
8/8/6R1/8/1b6/8/k1K5/8 w - - 0 1	17.188
8/8/8/8/8/1Q1K1k2/3B4/8 w - - 0 1	12.5
8/K7/8/1b6/1k6/8/2QP4/8 w - - 0 1	11.719
3Q4/2b5/8/8/1p4K1/8/8/5k2 w - - 0 1	13.281
7k/4p3/2R5/8/3R4/4Kp2/8/6n1 w - - 0 1	18.75
8/1pK2B2/7k/8/1B6/1n6/8/1R6 w - - 0 1	21.875
8/4k3/1Rp5/2K2BN1/5p2/8/4p3/3R4 w - - 0 1	25
4b3/p4k1K/8/2B5/8/Q7/8/8 w - - 0 1	21.094
1kN4b/8/K3R3/8/1r6/p7/8/2R5 w - - 0 1	19.531
2k5/4p3/6PP/1n5K/n5R1/q2p4/b6R/5B2 w - - 0 1	28.125
RB6/4K2k/8/1B6/8/7n/8/8 w - - 0 1	25
8/7B/7k/8/6K1/8/R7/8 w - - 0 1	13.281
8/1B6/6K1/1R3R2/k3p3/8/2P5/q2N1n2 w - - 0 1	21.875
3K4/4n3/8/8/1nN1pP1Q/3N2R1/4kq2 w - - 0 1	30.469
5B2/4n3/3R4/6R1/4p1Q1/k4B2/2r5/7K w - - 0 1	27.344
8/8/2p3Qp/1r4N1/2KB4/8/6k1/1B5r w - - 0 1	26.562
1bR5/n7/8/Kp4k1/1N1B4/Q7/P7/r1n5 w - - 0 1	26.562
8/8/2R5/6B1/8/3K2k1/8/8 w - - 0 1	22.656
7k/5K2/8/8/5b2/8/2R5/8 w - - 0 1	12.5
4R2q/8/8/K7/8/1k6/8/3R4 w - - 0 1	11.719

R7/8/3P4/3k4/8/4K3/5B2/8 w - - 0 1	15.625
7q/7Q/2Pkp3/1K6/8/4B3/8/8 w - - 0 1	14.062
8/3K1N2/1p4k1/8/8/8/4R3/8 w - - 0 1	18.75
8/7K/n6p/8/k5P1/2B2p2/4Bp2/7R w - - 0 1	21.094
4Q3/8/8/n1p5/4K3/8/4p3/6k1 w - - 0 1	22.656
8/8/3p4/8/2K5/N7/2pB4/k7 w - - 0 1	18.75
3R4/4K1p1/7b/4N3/k7/1N5R/8/8 w - - 0 1	21.875
3K4/8/8/1R6/8/1Q1P1k2/p7/8 w - - 0 1	17.188
K7/1N2B3/k7/N7/8/6Rb/8/8 w - - 0 1	20.312
4K3/Q2N4/8/6rk/5B2/8/8/8 w - - 0 1	20.312
8/6Np/1p6/k3P3/P3N2b/8/K3B3/8 w - - 0 1	25
8/1B2NK2/1k6/8/8/8/n1Q5/8 w - - 0 1	20.312
7k/6b1/5N2/8/1K6/8/6q1/2Q5 w - - 0 1	18.75
2k1B3/2pp4/p1P2K2/8/8/7n/7p/7R w - - 0 1	22.656
1K1kq3/1b6/8/3N4/2R5/Q7/8/8 w - - 0 1	24.219
3k1q2/5Q2/8/2N5/8/5KR1/2n5/8 w - - 0 1	18.75
2k5/1R6/8/8/n7/2r1P3/2Q5/3B3K w - - 0 1	21.094
8/8/8/3K1p2/8/1N5R/Nk6/8 w - - 0 1	21.875
3q4/r7/5QRK/8/8/8/N1r2p2/2Nk4 w - - 0 1	21.875
4n3/2q5/8/QK6/4R3/1b6/1k6/n3N3 w - - 0 1	29.688
7b/5P2/8/K7/5N1k/8/8/6R1 w - - 0 1	21.094
2k4b/BNp2R2/4K2R/2P5/2n5/8/8/8 w - - 0 1	19.531
7Q/8/8/1pK5/8/8/8/3kB3 w - - 0 1	18.75
8/8/2R5/6Q1/7K/5k2/4p1b1/8 w - - 0 1	17.188
3B4/Kp6/7Q/5b2/k3n3/8/7R/N3r3 w - - 0 1	25
8/2KN1Q2/b1B5/8/8/2b5/7k/8 w - - 0 1	24.219
8/3K2p1/6Q1/8/1N6/k7/8/8 w - - 0 1	16.406
4k3/2p5/R7/5P2/2B5/8/8/5K2 w - - 0 1	17.188
k5K1/1p2QR2/8/6b1/8/B6p/1r6/8 w - - 0 1	23.438
8/8/7k/8/1R2BP1p/8/8/1K6 w - - 0 1	23.438
2B1R3/8/K2p4/6R1/k4N2/8/3p4/8 w - - 0 1	19.531
8/8/N2r1R2/2R1p3/2nk4/8/4P3/6KQ w - - 0 1	23.438
1r6/6n1/6K1/4k3/4N3/R7/8/5Q2 w - - 0 1	24.219
3Q4/5k2/2K5/8/8/p7/8/7B w - - 0 1	16.406
7k/7p/4K3/8/3b4/8/p3R3/8 w - - 0 1	17.188
5Q2/8/6n1/8/8/8/R2p3K/4k3 w - - 0 1	16.406

```
k7/1b6/7R/2K5/8/8/8/8 w - - 0 1                      15.625
2k5/n7/7K/8/2p2B1Q/1BN5/8/8 w - - 0 1                16.406
1n1B4/2R5/5K1k/8/8/4p3/8/8 w - - 0 1                 19.531
8/6K1/2b5/7k/8/Q5P1/8/8 w - - 0 1                    17.188
8/1R6/4Q3/8/8/2nnK3/2p5/3k4 w - - 0 1                18.75
8/1n5k/8/6K1/8/8/1R6/8 w - - 0 1                     14.844
8/8/2k5/8/3b4/1Q2N1K1/5R2/1q4n1 w - - 0 1            18.75
7k/1P2K3/1b6/8/8/8/6R1/r7 w - - 0 1                  21.875
4k3/8/3R4/p7/2K5/8/6N1/2R4r w - - 0 1                17.969
k4K2/ppb5/2Pp4/8/2Q5/8/8/8 w - - 0 1                 18.75
1n5R/8/4k3/3p1r2/1Q2p1B1/8/5B2/6K1 w - - 0 1         28.125
8/K4R2/8/8/3R4/k3N3/2r5/8 w - - 0 1                  25
8/4b3/8/8/3K4/N5Q1/1k6/8 w - - 0 1                   12.5
8/5n2/6kp/8/5K2/2B5/3n4/Q7 w - - 0 1                 18.75
8/4K3/8/1R4B1/P1k5/5N2/8/8 w - - 0 1                 20.312
8/4Kb2/4p2k/3r3p/8/4N1Q1/8/8 w - - 0 1               18.75
8/6np/3R4/8/pp1K4/k2n4/3B2Q1/8 w - - 0 1             28.125
2r5/1bR5/8/5R2/k7/8/8/K3B3 w - - 0 1                 24.219
8/8/8/8/5P1k/8/1K3N2/1Q2n3 w - - 0 1                 17.969
1b6/8/KB6/7Q/7R/3pp3/1kB5/3b4 w - - 0 1              20.312
1B6/1k6/2n5/1p6/5Q2/4K1p1/4R3/8 w - - 0 1            23.438
7k/2n3r1/8/5P2/5K2/8/6R1/5Q2 w - - 0 1               21.094
5QK1/8/6k1/8/8/8/R7/6q1 w - - 0 1                    18.75
8/Q2R4/3N4/6K1/8/2k5/8/5n2 w - - 0 1                 17.188
8/8/2p5/8/1R6/5K2/3p4/3Bk3 w - - 0 1                 18.75
8/5r2/q4Q2/8/4B3/2K5/8/2k5 w - - 0 1                 18.75
8/8/8/k7/8/8/1K2BR2/8 w - - 0 1                      15.625
4nk2/8/8/6K1/6Q1/8/8/8 w - - 0 1                     12.5
1K6/8/2p1R3/4B3/B3Q3/k3n3/8/8 w - - 0 1              18.75
3R1K2/1R5p/1b5k/1B6/8/2B5/p7/r7 w - - 0 1            28.125
6nk/5R2/8/6K1/8/8/8/8 w - - 0 1                      21.875
4R3/2K5/8/1k6/8/4N3/8/8 w - - 0 1                    12.5
8/4Q2q/3r4/8/1bK5/3N4/8/k7 w - - 0 1                 17.188
8/2R4Q/1B6/1k5K/1r2b3/1q6/8/8 w - - 0 1              18.75
7R/8/8/8/8/K7/4B3/1k2n3 w - - 0 1                    20.312
2k5/K7/1Q6/7b/8/8/8/8 w - - 0 1                      14.062
```

4k3/1BK1B3/8/8/8/8/3p3R/8 w - - 0 1	15.625
1R6/8/8/kN6/8/1P5K/8/3n4 w - - 0 1	18.75
8/7R/R7/8/8/b1K5/k4p2/7q w - - 0 1	20.312
Q3Kb1k/8/8/8/8/8/8/7n w - - 0 1	16.406
3K4/8/6p1/6P1/5B1k/3Q3P/5nP1/1bq5 w - - 0 1	25
5k2/8/3K4/1B6/8/3b3R/R1n3n1/8 w - - 0 1	22.656
8/4p3/6k1/5N2/4R3/8/2pQK3/8 w - - 0 1	21.094
8/8/K7/7B/R3N2p/6p1/5R2/2r1k3 w - - 0 1	22.656
q7/8/8/5Q2/2rB2K1/4p3/8/7k w - - 0 1	25
6R1/4K3/3R4/7k/8/5P2/6P1/rn6 w - - 0 1	23.438
7Q/1b5N/8/5k2/4R3/1K6/8/6q1 w - - 0 1	23.438
k6b/2Q5/8/7q/8/6K1/7B/8 w - - 0 1	17.969
1Rr3B1/4k1p1/5N2/7N/5B2/2P5/1b4K1/8 w - - 0 1	24.219
R3K3/3p3k/8/8/8/n7/8/R7 w - - 0 1	26.562
8/k7/8/7p/8/8/8/N1K1Q3 w - - 0 1	14.844
2B5/k7/2K5/1P6/8/8/p7/8 w - - 0 1	12.5
8/5K1k/5nr1/Q7/8/8/8/8 w - - 0 1	15.625
6K1/3R4/4k1b1/2p5/7N/2Q5/8/4b1nB w - - 0 1	21.094
8/7p/2Q5/8/7k/3p4/3K4/8 w - - 0 1	21.094
8/8/8/8/8/k7/1p1KQ3/4N3 w - - 0 1	12.5
8/6p1/4Q3/2N5/2P2k1p/1K6/5P2/8 w - - 0 1	20.312
2K5/1N5Q/8/3kp2q/8/6B1/1R6/4b1n1 w - - 0 1	28.125
4N3/8/8/8/5N1K/b1pB4/8/6k1 w - - 0 1	24.219
8/1r6/8/k3p3/1R3Qn1/6K1/8/8 w - - 0 1	19.531
6R1/1B1b4/1B1kp3/K1N5/2r3RN/8/8/8 w - - 0 1	21.094
8/3n4/3R4/5K2/2k5/1N6/8/7Q w - - 0 1	19.531
3k4/8/2p5/8/4N3/6R1/6K1/1B6 w - - 0 1	18.75
1B4N1/5k2/1K6/R7/1b2n2R/Q4P1B/4q3/3b4 w - - 0 1	27.344
8/3p4/2p5/2K1N3/8/1B3p1k/1Q6/8 w - - 0 1	28.125
8/1B2p2K/2q1N3/8/2r5/3N4/8/1Q4Bk w - - 0 1	25.781
8/b7/3N4/8/2K2Q1N/1B3n1k/8/8 w - - 0 1	25.781
2Q5/8/6b1/8/N7/8/8/1k5K w - - 0 1	20.312
1k1K4/b1N1p2Q/8/2p5/8/1b2R1q1/8/8 w - - 0 1	23.438
1kN5/3R4/8/8/6K1/4P3/4r2p/7B w - - 0 1	22.656
7R/8/kN1K1n2/p7/8/8/2P5/r7 w - - 0 1	25
8/2P5/8/3K2R1/8/8/8/2b4k w - - 0 1	20.312

```
1k6/8/3q4/p2NRQ2/R7/8/8/1K6 w - - 0 1                        17.969
1K6/8/Q7/8/8/6p1/1k6/5N2 w - - 0 1                           17.969
2k2r2/5B2/NB5R/2K5/4b3/8/8/7R w - - 0 1                      19.531
8/6p1/3Pp1P1/8/6K1/8/8/7k w - - 0 1                          21.094
2n5/3P4/1R5r/6k1/KR6/8/8/3n4 w - - 0 1                       21.875
7n/QN1nk2N/6P1/3p3R/1K6/8/3pB3/5nq1 w - - 0 1                29.688
2N2k2/3RN3/R4b2/5r1P/8/2b1K3/8/1Q3b2 w - - 0 1               31.25
1Q6/5B1K/8/4Pk2/6b1/2P1pP2/6p1/4B3 w - - 0 1                 28.906
k7/5R2/8/8/Nb6/5N2/4K3/8 w - - 0 1                           21.875
3K4/3N2k1/8/7p/1R6/r7/5Q2/8 w - - 0 1                        17.969
8/7k/1Q6/8/8/2K3B1/8/2b5 w - - 0 1                           18.75
5K2/8/k7/2Q5/5n2/r4B2/4R3/8 w - - 0 1                        18.75
1k3r2/3Q4/8/2P5/3p4/8/5P2/3K4 w - - 0 1                      17.188
K1R5/3N4/7k/8/2N5/6p1/8/8 w - - 0 1                          17.969
8/8/p6K/8/5RBB/8/8/2k5 w - - 0 1                             16.406
K7/8/8/4N2r/8/3N2k1/3R2p1/1Q6 w - - 0 1                      21.875
3b4/4R3/1N6/n7/8/k7/2QK4/8 w - - 0 1                         21.094
7k/8/4K3/8/8/R7/6n1/8 w - - 0 1                              14.844
N7/8/8/kP6/8/3K4/3p4/6R1 w - - 0 1                           15.625
r3k3/1pp5/4Kp2/2pp4/2N2p2/2Q5/6p1/8 w q - 0 1                25.781
3bR3/8/8/8/5p2/NBBk1pN1/8/K7 w - - 0 1                       26.562
8/1Kp5/3B4/2R5/8/7k/p2R4/8 w - - 0 1                         26.562
3B2bk/4Q3/6K1/7n/8/8/5q2/8 w - - 0 1                         21.875
4Q2K/8/4B3/8/8/5kN1/8/8 w - - 0 1                            16.406
4K3/pp6/5p2/8/8/4k3/P2NP3/4QR1b w - - 0 1                    22.656
8/5P2/8/p6k/4B3/4K3/2r5/8 w - - 0 1                          24.219
2K5/8/Q7/1q2N2B/3n1k2/B7/1R6/7R w - - 0 1                    22.656
1B3nb1/4R3/3QR3/2p5/1p6/5K2/k2N4/1r5 w - - 0 1               34.375
6k1/R2B4/2R1r3/8/1q5b/8/8/K4N2 w - - 0 1                     25.781
8/8/4R3/4K3/8/8/3k4/3B4 w - - 0 1                            17.969
6k1/8/7B/7N/8/2K5/8/4Rn2 w - - 0 1                           15.625
8/3R2Q1/8/K6R/8/4kp2/2r5/1r6 w - - 0 1                       19.531
4Nk2/7K/8/8/1N3n1p/p6Q/8/6B1 w - - 0 1                       26.562
1kn5/1p6/1P5N/3p4/8/8/K5R1 w - - 0 1                         24.219
8/8/1K2R3/6kB/2R5/7n/1B6/8 w - - 0 1                         21.094
7K/R7/2b5/8/8/7R/8/3k4 w - - 0 1                             16.406
```

8/8/1Q2b3/8/8/1r2Pn2/k7/2K5 w - - 0 1	18.75
2K5/k7/8/1n6/6R1/8/8/4Bn2 w - - 0 1	20.312
2n4Q/7p/4K1np/1kP2N2/qp6/R7/B2P4/5b2 w - - 0 1	25.781
8/5Q2/8/8/b7/8/1pk5/4K2R w - - 0 1	30.469
8/8/8/6p1/QK6/5p2/8/2k5 w - - 0 1	14.844
6B1/B5k1/3b4/1Q6/8/8/7P/2K5 w - - 0 1	16.406
8/2nb4/2N5/8/8/8/7Q/k5K1 w - - 0 1	17.969
7k/8/4K3/R7/7n/8/8/8 w - - 0 1	15.625
8/b7/8/8/8/2R1R3/3K4/3B1k2 w - - 0 1	15.625
3B2B1/8/4N3/8/n7/4NK2/3k1N2/8 w - - 0 1	17.188
K2k4/8/3Pr3/8/7R/Q4B2/1b6/8 w - - 0 1	17.969
8/8/8/4K3/1B6/1k2PQ2/6P1/8 w - - 0 1	19.531
8/2b5/Q2N4/p1K5/2R5/1k6/2b5/8 w - - 0 1	18.75
8/8/6BK/4B3/6k1/8/n7/2R5 w - - 0 1	21.875
1R6/P7/4n3/8/8/8/2k3P1/4K3 w - - 0 1	18.75
5R2/8/2q5/1B1NK3/5Q2/n3p3/2r5/3k4 w - - 0 1	22.656
1k3K2/8/8/8/2B5/5n2/8/2Q5 w - - 0 1	21.094
2qk4/8/8/4R3/8/K1B1n3/4Q3/6R1 w - - 0 1	20.312
5R2/B6p/8/K6N/6k1/8/4R3/2n5 w - - 0 1	22.656
8/8/3Q4/8/3K4/8/n7/4k3 w - - 0 1	18.75
8/8/5B1r/8/8/1K6/2N1P1k1/1Q6 w - - 0 1	17.188
8/5p1k/8/8/4R3/4N3/1K6/7B w - - 0 1	20.312
6R1/8/5b2/8/8/8/3KB3/k7 w - - 0 1	17.188
8/8/8/n6n/8/K1N4R/8/B1k2B2 w - - 0 1	17.969
6n1/3K4/8/8/k7/7R/2N5/8 w - - 0 1	17.188
5K2/8/7n/5P1k/4b2N/6Q1/8/8 w - - 0 1	18.75
4N1k1/1K6/8/B4R2/8/8/8/5b2 w - - 0 1	17.969
4k3/8/3K4/R2p4/8/r1R5/Q2p4/8 w - - 0 1	17.188
8/4Np2/5k1K/6n1/6pR/8/3R4/8 w - - 0 1	22.656
8/8/8/4N3/4N3/5B1n/k1K5/8 w - - 0 1	21.875
2k5/8/7b/8/4N3/Q3P3/4K3/8 w - - 0 1	15.625
8/2q4P/8/8/8/1R6/4K3/k7 w - - 0 1	14.062
8/5pK1/8/6k1/rr6/2Q3P1/8/6RB w - - 0 1	21.875
8/6b1/8/6k1/8/1R4pQ/7R/1n5K w - - 0 1	16.406
8/8/3K4/2R5/8/8/4k3/3N2R1 w - - 0 1	20.312
8/8/6Q1/5K2/7k/6p1/8/3b4 w - - 0 1	13.281

FEN	Value
8/8/2Q5/b7/4K3/6B1/3k1N2/8 w - - 0 1	14.844
3K4/1p6/1N1k4/8/R3r1r1/5p2/B7/4Q3 w - - 0 1	22.656
8/4Q3/5Np1/8/6pn/6k1/8/1K5R w - - 0 1	25.781
2b5/8/8/3pQ3/K5n1/8/7B/1k6 w - - 0 1	18.75
4K3/7k/6R1/8/n7/8/8/6B1 w - - 0 1	16.406
4N2K/1p1k4/8/8/8/5B2/2n4Q w - - 0 1	16.406
8/8/8/4N3/4R3/k7/2K5/4b3 w - - 0 1	18.75
8/b7/5Q2/6R1/8/8/4Kpb1/6k1 w - - 0 1	18.75
3q4/1Q6/7R/5kp1/6r1/2K5/8/8 w - - 0 1	19.531
7r/2b5/8/2Q5/4p3/4N1k1/8/B4K2 w - - 0 1	23.438
3k4/7Q/2p3P1/5n2/3p4/6R1/1p6/2b4K w - - 0 1	25.781
2N5/5k2/7K/8/8/8/8/R7 w - - 0 1	21.875
K2k4/8/1R6/Np3Q2/p1rr4/7p/2p5/2b5 w - - 0 1	25
8/5P2/6P1/8/8/8/2k1K3 w - - 0 1	22.656
4K1Bq/p4p2/5RPk/6r1/5Bp1/8/5P2/Q7 w - - 0 1	21.094
6r1/5P2/8/6bK/1N1Rp3/1k6/8/8 w - - 0 1	25.781
4k3/5p2/3R3R/p5p1/2K2p2/1P6/8/6N1 w - - 0 1	21.094
3k3K/4N1B1/8/8/2n5/8/B1p3QP/8 w - - 0 1	27.344
1n4q1/4B1p1/6Q1/8/8/7p/7k/K7 w - - 0 1	19.531
5k2/1B6/8/8/8/2R3K1/1R5p/8 w - - 0 1	19.531
8/8/7n/2pk4/2N5/1B6/6K1/Q7 w - - 0 1	20.312
8/2P5/K7/6P1/2B2B2/8/2n5/3k4 w - - 0 1	19.531
8/8/2k5/K4B2/3PnQ2/1R6/6q1/8 w - - 0 1	21.094
4K3/1P6/k7/7P/8/1pp2R2/8/1b6 w - - 0 1	22.656
8/k1KQ4/8/8/7q/8/8/8 w - - 0 1	18.75
7n/8/6R1/K7/8/8/R7/1k6 w - - 0 1	14.062
k1N1K3/8/8/8/5R2/8/8/8 w - - 0 1	14.062
8/8/k1N5/8/1K6/6R1/8/8 w - - 0 1	12.5
3nk3/2P3P1/5K2/8/4b3/8/4P3/8 w - - 0 1	17.188
8/8/8/k1K4Q/8/8/3n4/8 w - - 0 1	17.188
8/8/1r2P3/5P2/2bB3K/6pp/6kr/3NQ3 w - - 0 1	25
8/8/7K/8/3R2N1/7k/8/3rQ3 w - - 0 1	17.969
8/5r2/8/8/6Kp/1Q6/8/7k w - - 0 1	14.844
5r2/2b5/3k2K1/8/2R5/2Q5/8/8 w - - 0 1	17.188
q1n1Bk2/8/1R3K2/3p2N1/8/2p5/8/8 w - - 0 1	18.75
8/Rp6/2B5/8/8/4k3/2K2R2/8 w - - 0 1	23.438

8/6B1/8/8/1Q1K4/5k2/2B3N1/7b w - - 0 1	17.969
3B4/5Q1p/8/1p5P/4p3/2Kp4/6k1/8 w - - 0 1	22.656
kB6/8/N2K4/3P4/2p5/8/8/8 w - - 0 1	23.438
3nQ1B1/5p2/8/8/6k1/8/8/4B2K w - - 0 1	20.312
1q2B3/2k3r1/2p1K3/8/8/8/5B2/3Q4 w - - 0 1	21.094
8/5K2/7k/7p/7n/8/2Q5/8 w - - 0 1	20.312
8/4N3/2K5/8/7k/8/4N3/4R3 w - - 0 1	13.281
4k2K/8/8/B3p3/4R3/7R/2p5/8 w - - 0 1	18.75
8/2pk4/1B6/4K2Q/8/8/8/8 w - - 0 1	16.406
3b4/1n6/3kBQ2/8/8/1N6/7K/R7 w - - 0 1	20.312
7R/7B/8/8/8/2b4k/5K2 w - - 0 1	17.969
8/3b3N/4Q2p/7k/8/7K/8 w - - 0 1	12.5
8/8/8/8/3K4/B7/1R6/3kb3 w - - 0 1	17.188
8/2R5/8/8/8/pK3R2/1P2p3/4k3 w - - 0 1	11.719
8/3p2k1/3R4/6p1/7p/8/7K/1R6 w - - 0 1	21.875
5QB1/5K2/6r1/2b5/4k3/6R1/1Q6/4n3 w - - 0 1	25
1N6/k7/8/8/5K2/8/6p1/5Q2 w - - 0 1	21.875
8/8/5K2/8/5k2/2N4R/8/8 w - - 0 1	11.719
3B1r2/1R6/8/KQ3p2/3k4/3N4/1Pn5/n7 w - - 0 1	23.438
3K2Bk/2p5/5P2/2bPn3/6p1/5Q2/8/8 w - - 0 1	30.469
4N1b1/4R3/1KP1r3/3k2p1/8/2B5/1n6/4Q3 w - - 0 1	28.125
1k6/8/B7/4n3/4pp2/B7/4K3/1n2N2Q w - - 0 1	30.469
8/8/5K2/8/2R5/8/7n/k1n3R1 w - - 0 1	25
8/5k1K/8/8/3B3R/8/8/8 w - - 0 1	15.625
1K3BN1/7k/8/8/8/5p2/1R6/8 w - - 0 1	13.281
1K6/8/8/Qp6/n7/7p/3R4/r6k w - - 0 1	18.75
8/8/8/7p/3B1k1P/qB6/1b5K/Q1N5 w - - 0 1	25.781
8/8/7n/8/6Bk/Q3K3/8/8 w - - 0 1	18.75
8/6Q1/1K6/6nN/8/7k/4B1r1/R7 w - - 0 1	20.312
8/8/1Q6/2p5/k7/8/8/4K2b w - - 0 1	17.969
k7/2q5/K7/8/8/8/Q7/8 w - - 0 1	14.062
3Nk3/4P3/3q4/8/7K/3Q4/4rR2/8 w - - 0 1	18.75
8/8/7K/q7/1B5p/5p1b/5Qnk/8 w - - 0 1	21.875
5kB1/8/8/4R3/1b4R1/1K6/8/7b w - - 0 1	22.656
8/3k2N1/1P3p2/1K6/8/1bb1Q3/1B6/8 w - - 0 1	22.656
8/6k1/8/3K4/8/8/8/3B3R w - - 0 1	17.969

FEN	Value
8/8/K3RR2/2r5/6N1/6p1/6r1/7k w - - 0 1	16.406
3q4/8/3B4/8/8/Nr6/k2K2R1/8 w - - 0 1	21.094
5nr1/p7/6Nk/1K6/R7/2Q5/8/8 w - - 0 1	23.438
8/3b4/8/8/1B6/1B1K4/8/1k3N2 w - - 0 1	21.875
1K6/8/5p2/7k/8/2R5/3Q4/5n2 w - - 0 1	16.406
k7/5nQ1/2p5/8/8/4K3/2p5/4R3 w - - 0 1	20.312
8/2K5/k5P1/5R2/8/8/8/6n1 w - - 0 1	18.75
2R5/k1K1b3/8/P7/2N5/1r1Q1r2/8/8 w - - 0 1	18.75
4R2N/6P1/5p1K/7P/1P4p1/P7/bNkr2p1/6r1 w - - 0 1	37.5
8/p7/1k3N2/8/QP5b/8/1K6/8 w - - 0 1	26.562
k4n2/8/6Q1/1N6/6p1/K7/8/2r5 w - - 0 1	21.875
3B4/3p4/8/3R1N2/6R1/rp3k2/2N5/6K1 w - - 0 1	21.875
8/8/8/k1K5/P7/1B6/7q/7R w - - 0 1	22.656
7K/4r3/k2N4/8/8/B6p/8/6R1 w - - 0 1	20.312
8/2K5/8/2k5/1N6/8/8/6R1 w - - 0 1	14.062
6B1/8/3B2k1/5p1p/2KQ4/8/5r2/6n1 w - - 0 1	17.969
2K2N1k/8/3B1q2/5P1r/8/1B6/3bN3/8 w - - 0 1	21.875
6RQ/8/5p2/8/8/4KR1P/1q5k/8 w - - 0 1	23.438
8/5K2/n6N/1Q6/8/8/6nN/6k1 w - - 0 1	21.094
4K3/1kB5/R2R4/8/8/2r5/5N2/8 w - - 0 1	19.531
8/8/3Q4/2K5/8/k7/5p1p/8 w - - 0 1	14.062
8/5R2/1n6/8/8/B7/1PK4b/k7 w - - 0 1	14.062
7R/8/n7/8/4K2p/5N2/8/7k w - - 0 1	20.312
k7/1p5b/BbN4R/6b1/8/2Q2K2/8/8 w - - 0 1	20.312
1k6/8/1K6/5pr1/r7/8/8/6Q1 w - - 0 1	20.312
8/8/8/Q2P4/7k/5K2/8/b7 w - - 0 1	17.188
7R/4k3/5RP1/8/8/7K/8/B1r5 w - - 0 1	16.406
8/8/7p/3n3k/3K4/Q6P/8/8 w - - 0 1	17.969
8/1n4Q1/1R6/8/kp6/8/8/1K2b3 w - - 0 1	20.312
8/2R5/N5K1/1k6/8/4Rq2/6b1/4Q3 w - - 0 1	21.094
2NrR3/3k4/6R1/6K1/8/4B3/8/8 w - - 0 1	18.75
k3n3/P7/8/8/3R4/1B1p4/1K6/8 w - - 0 1	19.531
3K4/Pk6/5p2/8/R3b3/8/8/8 w - - 0 1	17.188
1K6/8/8/1B6/8/6N1/7k/R7 w - - 0 1	17.188
6nb/5N2/8/2n5/8/4N3/K3R3/6k1 w - - 0 1	20.312
2B5/8/3kn3/8/2KB1n2/7Q/8/8 w - - 0 1	23.438

k1N5/2K5/8/p7/2nR3n/3P3r/8/8 w - - 0 1	15.625
8/kp2KP2/2p5/8/2B5/8/8/8 w - - 0 1	21.094
4b3/4N3/2P5/B6r/3k4/K6Q/4P3/8 w - - 0 1	18.75
8/6K1/1kNP4/7r/8/4R3/5Q2/n7 w - - 0 1	21.094
8/8/3Q2pp/1RK3kb/8/8/8/8 w - - 0 1	18.75
8/3PpP2/1K1k4/8/8/4p3/8/8 w - - 0 1	17.969
1K5k/8/2q2Pp1/1Q6/8/2p5/8/8 w - - 0 1	20.312
K2k1B2/1p5b/8/4pp1n/8/8/5Q2/R7 w - - 0 1	26.562
n3K3/2R5/8/7k/8/8/8/1R6 w - - 0 1	18.75
4k3/pP6/2p5/R1b2B1K/1p6/8/8/R7 w - - 0 1	18.75
2q5/kp1QK3/8/8/1N6/2B5/8/8 w - - 0 1	19.531
7K/8/Q6b/8/4b3/7k/3p2R1/8 w - - 0 1	21.875
8/8/5Q2/k7/3K4/8/8/5n2 w - - 0 1	17.188
5b2/3r4/7Q/k7/3K4/8/6Q1/B7 w - - 0 1	10.938
8/3b4/8/8/1p1R4/8/2K5/k7 w - - 0 1	11.719
k7/8/5B2/KR6/8/1b6/8/6n1 w - - 0 1	17.188
2R3Q1/k7/8/3q4/8/1R3b2/8/6K1 w - - 0 1	15.625
8/8/3p4/p7/k7/3N4/8/N1R1K3 w - - 0 1	21.875
8/7k/6r1/1B6/8/8/2PK4/8 w - - 0 1	18.75
3kr3/7K/3B4/8/8/4Q3/8/8 w - - 0 1	13.281
8/8/8/8/3B4/5B1K/8/5kN1 w - - 0 1	15.625
4KQ2/8/4B3/8/1p6/8/8/3k4 w - - 0 1	15.625
8/5P2/8/2p4b/1k6/8/2R5/4K3 w - - 0 1	14.844
8/2B5/8/3B4/3P4/2p3K1/8/knb2Q2 w - - 0 1	23.438
2k5/8/1K1n4/8/4Q3/8/8/8 w - - 0 1	20.312
8/6K1/2b5/8/3B4/6P1/4Q3/5n1k w - - 0 1	17.188
7R/rk6/b6K/8/8/8/7Q/8 w - - 0 1	20.312
8/8/5k1K/3b4/8/Q6N/8/7B w - - 0 1	15.625
1Q1B4/8/8/2k5/6K1/8/8/8 w - - 0 1	15.625
6Bk/p7/8/8/1R6/5K2/6p1/4N3 w - - 0 1	17.188
1k6/8/2R2K2/8/4R3/8/8/4q3 w - - 0 1	16.406
8/6R1/7K/8/1n2n3/8/8/4N2k w - - 0 1	12.5
3b4/2P5/1rk5/2Nr4/2K5/5N2/8/8 w - - 0 1	21.875
8/1p1Q3b/q7/1p6/3K3k/B3P3/8/1B2R3 w - - 0 1	29.688
BR6/3N4/3k3N/3P2p1/4q3/K7/7r/4Q3 w - - 0 1	27.344
8/8/8/5K2/4nB2/2R5/k7/8 w - - 0 1	22.656

```
1k6/8/8/8/1b6/8/4B2K/7Q w - - 0 1                        15.625
8/3r1B2/8/8/5R2/2K5/8/4k3 w - - 0 1                      15.625
8/8/7R/5Qn1/8/3K2k1/4r2b/8 w - - 0 1                     18.75
2n3K1/1r2k3/8/1R6/6Q1/1r6/8/8 w - - 0 1                  21.875
8/N7/8/k1p5/4NK2/3R4/8/8 w - - 0 1                       20.312
3N4/3K4/8/3b4/8/8/R3r2R/1k6 w - - 0 1                    20.312
K1k5/3n4/1P6/2pn2Q1/6N1/8/8/8 w - - 0 1                  18.75
8/3P4/n7/8/8/5K2/7k/8 w - - 0 1                          16.406
8/8/3b4/8/2B5/7Q/5k2/3K4 w - - 0 1                       14.062
8/3P4/7K/5p2/8/k7/3B4/8 w - - 0 1                        15.625
7n/2K5/8/1rRN3R/8/8/1p6/kN6 w - - 0 1                    21.875
5q2/1K6/4R3/2k5/4r3/3Q4/8/8 w - - 0 1                    21.094
8/K6P/p3p2R/k1P2bb1/1R6/1P1N1n2/8/2rN4 w - - 0 1         25.781
8/1N2bR2/8/5q2/k1K5/1R6/8/8 w - - 0 1                    29.688
2Q5/8/1b6/8/8/k1p5/8/2K5 w - - 0 1                       18.75
8/1P3B2/8/8/1K1k4/3N4/2P2b2/6b1 w - - 0 1                20.312
8/8/8/8/6p1/N7/1p2RK1k/8 w - - 0 1                       19.531
8/8/6K1/p2n4/r3N3/k7/3RN3/1R6 w - - 0 1                  18.75
8/3P4/1pN5/2R5/8/K7/3k4/8 w - - 0 1                      18.75
2Bk2K1/4p3/1R6/8/6p1/8/8/8 w - - 0 1                     16.406
3N2Qb/8/6b1/5p2/8/1K6/8/1k6 w - - 0 1                    15.625
8/4K3/3N4/7k/1R6/1p6/8/8 w - - 0 1                       16.406
8/8/8/8/k7/5N2/bK2Q3/8 w - - 0 1                         15.625
k1n3BK/P7/8/8/1N6/8/4bp2/5Qn1 w - - 0 1                  21.094
2B3Q1/k1p4p/8/8/8/1P2nK2/2p5/8 w - - 0 1                 22.656
8/2p3R1/rb1p4/8/8/Q2K4/5N1k/8 w - - 0 1                  25
8/R1r5/3Q4/2B5/4p2P/6bK/8/2n1Nr1k w - - 0 1              28.125
8/1r6/1N6/Q7/KN4p1/2k5/7B/8 w - - 0 1                    31.25
8/5R2/4p3/kN6/8/3N2K1/8/8 w - - 0 1                      19.531
5k1n/8/8/5N2/2Q2K2/8/8/8 w - - 0 1                       17.188
2R2B2/1r6/1k6/8/K7/8/5r2/8 w - - 0 1                     14.844
3R4/2n5/3P2R1/5k2/8/8/5K2/8 w - - 0 1                    16.406
1R6/8/3n2K1/4p3/8/3n2RN/7k/7N w - - 0 1                  18.75
1k6/8/2b5/1N1R4/8/8/8/1Q2K3 w - - 0 1                    21.094
2N5/2k2N1Q/2r5/R7/3K4/4Rq1r/b7/8 w - - 0 1               24.219
8/8/6K1/8/5k2/4r3/Q3R1B1/8 w - - 0 1                     21.875
```

1N1k4/8/8/8/1Q2K3/1B6/5q2/2B5 w - - 0 1	20.312
4R3/8/6q1/8/3pp3/3P4/1P1k4/1K1B3Q w - - 0 1	24.219
8/8/8/1K4R1/8/R7/1n4p1/4k3 w - - 0 1	22.656
6b1/p1N5/1kP5/3R4/8/K7/2R5/8 w - - 0 1	19.531
5Q2/rp1K3R/8/8/8/8/8/1k1N4 w - - 0 1	21.094
8/8/1Nk2p2/2P1P3/8/2KN4/8/8 w - - 0 1	21.875
4K3/7Q/3B4/5n2/N1RPk3/2q5/4brN1/8 w - - 0 1	27.344
k7/1n3K2/2p5/4R3/5n2/8/8/7Q w - - 0 1	29.688
8/8/6P1/8/8/7k/4B2P/5K2 w - - 0 1	18.75
8/4k3/3pP3/2b5/6K1/8/1Q6/8 w - - 0 1	17.188
7n/4R3/5Q2/3RKb2/2k5/8/2n5/8 w - - 0 1	19.531
8/8/1K2Q3/8/3R4/8/3b4/2k1N3 w - - 0 1	21.875
1n5k/8/8/6K1/8/8/8/4R3 w - - 0 1	13.281
1k6/2r5/8/8/R7/K7/3Q4/8 w - - 0 1	11.719
8/3K4/7k/8/8/5B2/3R4/8 w - - 0 1	11.719
1k6/1b6/3p4/K7/2Q5/8/8/8 w - - 0 1	14.062
8/8/k2N3n/8/6Q1/8/K7/8 w - - 0 1	13.281

Appendix C

Experimental Samples

In this section are all the computer-generated compositions (by Chesthetica) for the 'new and unseen' samples (NUS and NUS2) and 'baseline rejected' samples (BRS and BRS2) used in the experiments performed (refer chapter 5). The interested reader may want to compare them against their own personal preference or taste in chess problems or just attempt to solve them, hence the provided stipulation beneath each diagram. Each sample of 20 compositions is sequenced from left to right (e.g. 1, 2) before proceeding to the next row (e.g. 3, 4).

NUS

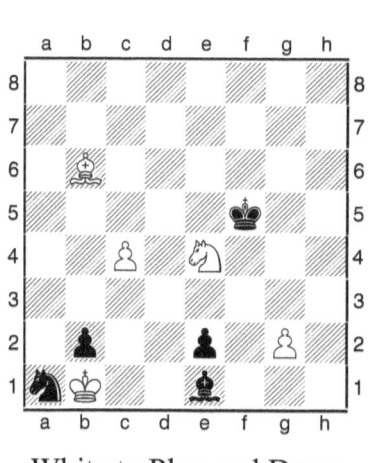

White to Play and Draw

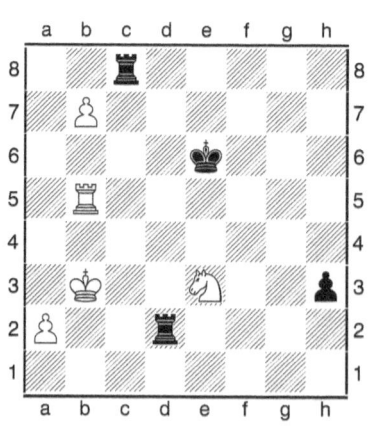

White to Play and Mate in 5

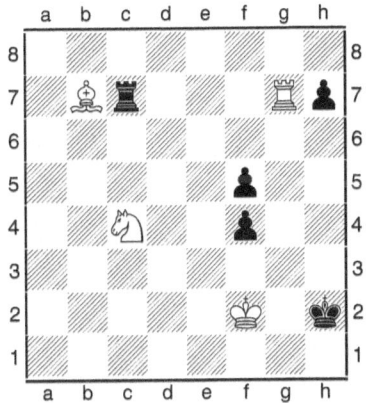

White to Play and Mate in 3

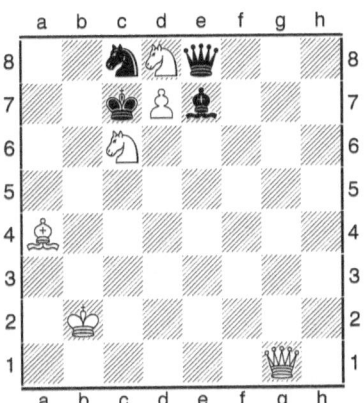

White to Play and Mate in 3

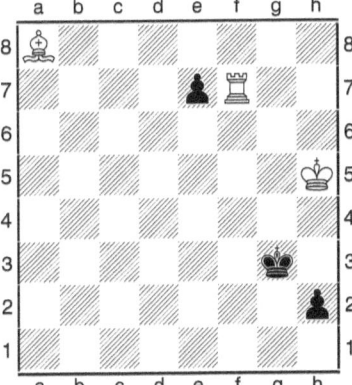

White to Play and Mate in 2

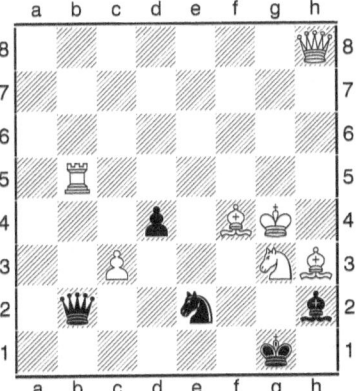

White to Play and Mate in 3

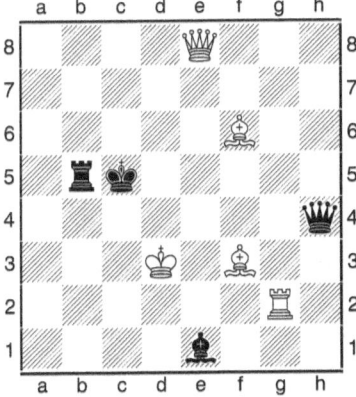

White to Play and Mate in 3

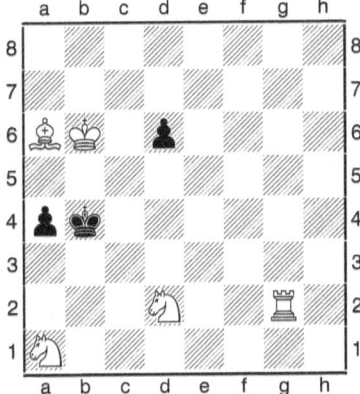

White to Play and Mate in 2

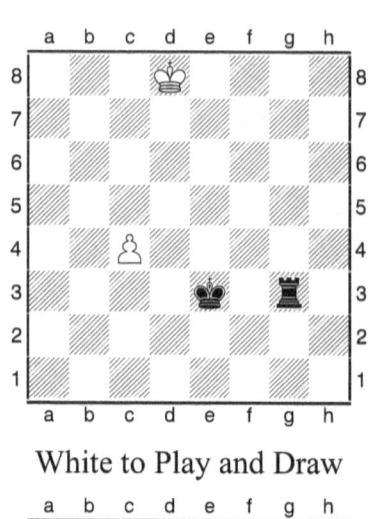

White to Play and Draw

White to Play and Mate in 3

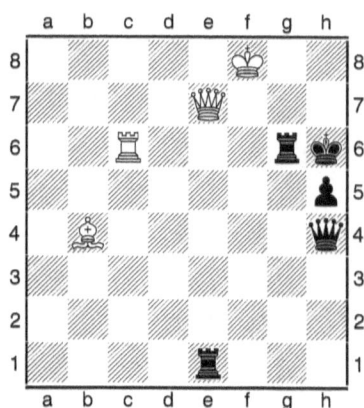

White to Play and Mate in 2

White to Play and Mate in 3

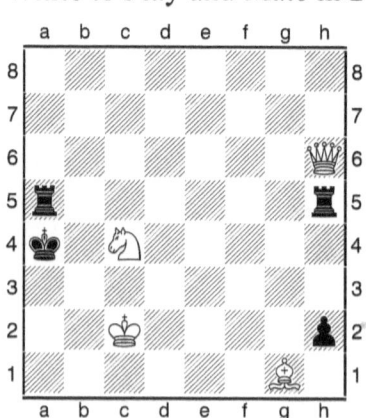

White to Play and Mate in 4

White to Play and Mate in 4

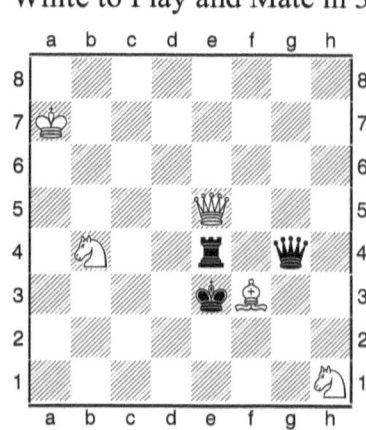

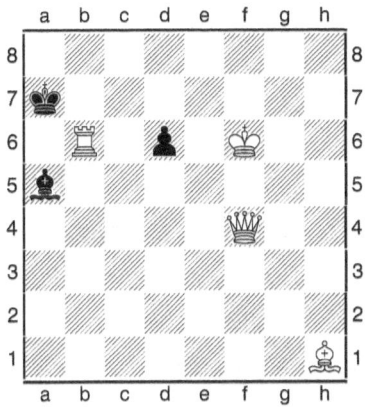

White to Play and Mate in 3

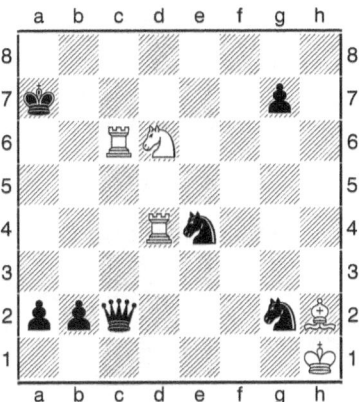

White to Play and Mate in 4

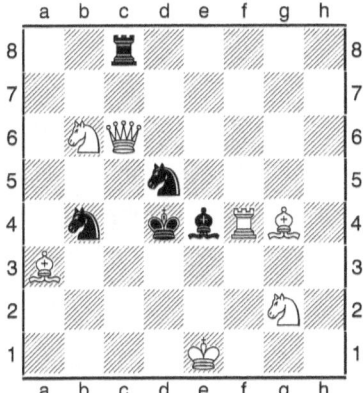

White to Play and Mate in 3

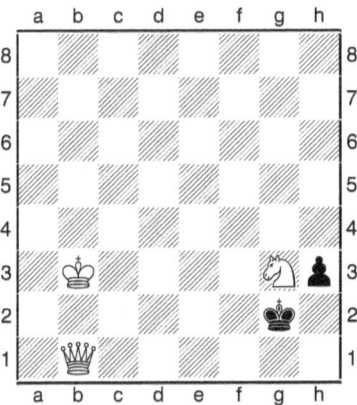

White to Play and Mate in 4

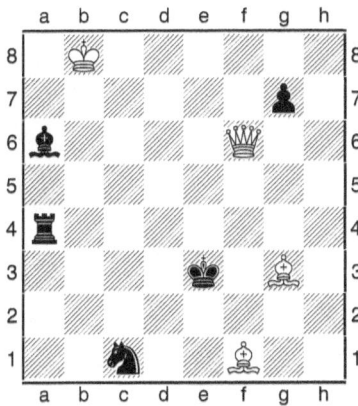

White to Play and Mate in 4

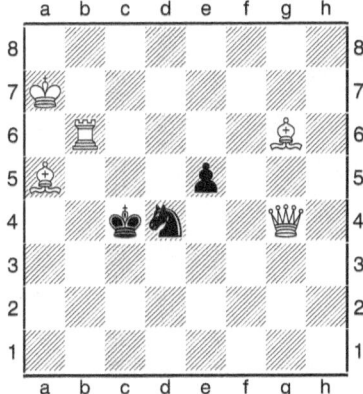

White to Play and Mate in 3

The second sample is NUS2. Instead of presenting the BRS ones, I believe grouping these two samples before the others makes more sense. Note that, chronologically, i.e. based on the dates these were generated, the following actually come *before* the NUS. The reason they are being presented here *after* the NUS is because they were used only in the second experiment to confirm the results obtained in the first.

NUS2

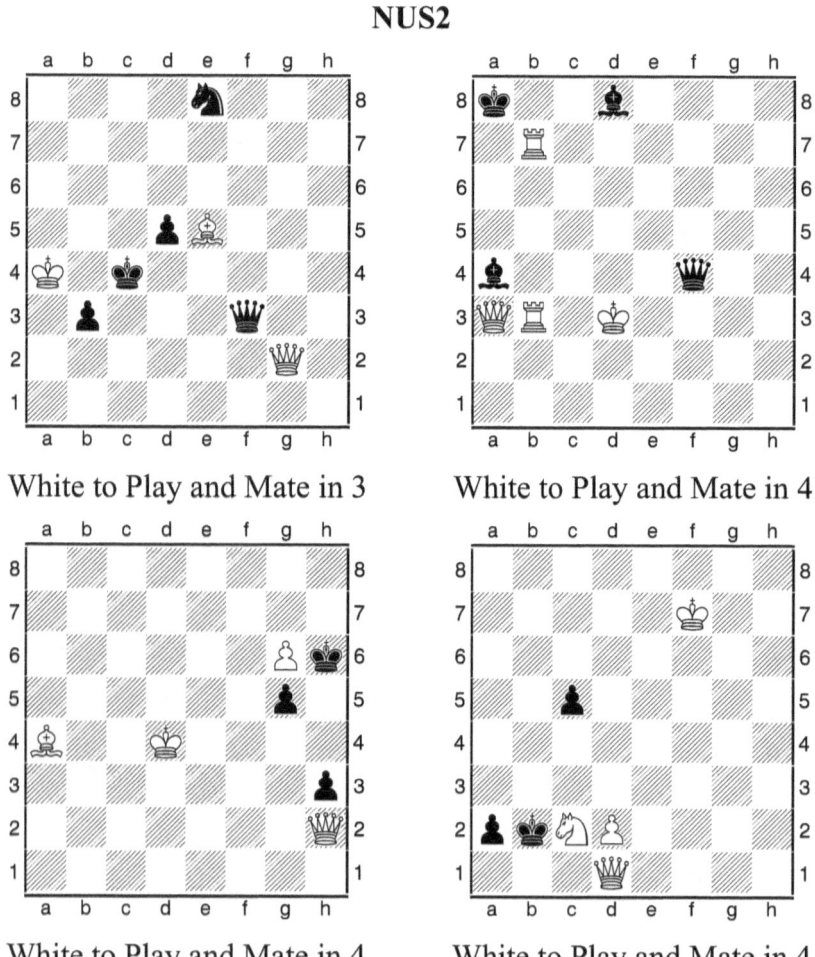

White to Play and Mate in 3

White to Play and Mate in 4

White to Play and Mate in 4

White to Play and Mate in 4

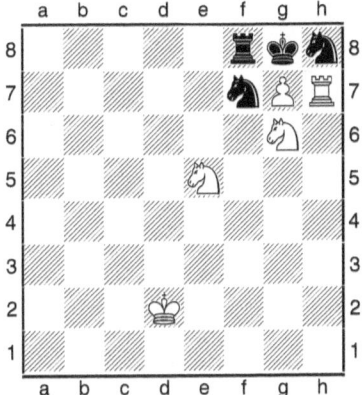

White to Play and Mate in 3

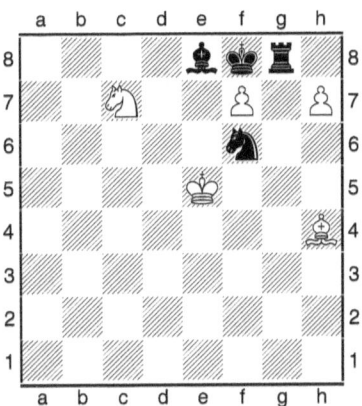

White to Play and Mate in 3

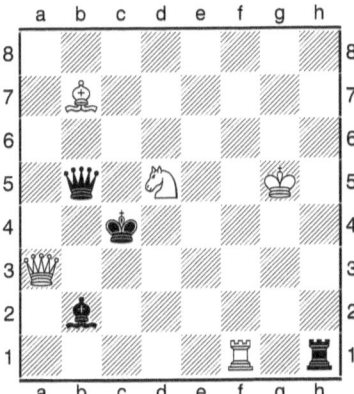

White to Play and Mate in 2

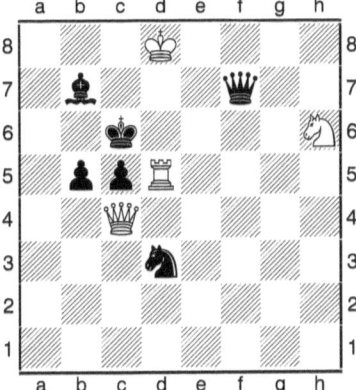

White to Play and Mate in 3

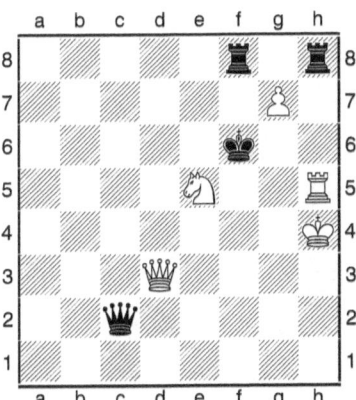

White to Play and Mate in 3

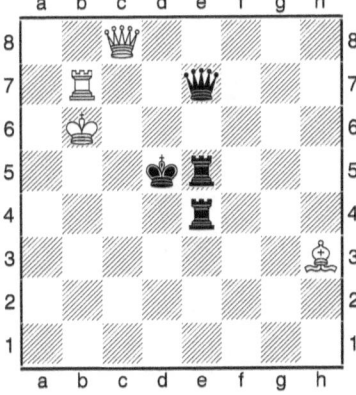

White to Play and Mate in 3

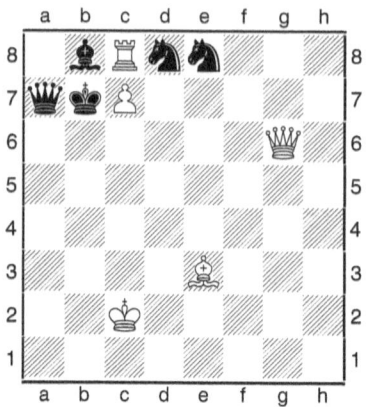

White to Play and Mate in 3

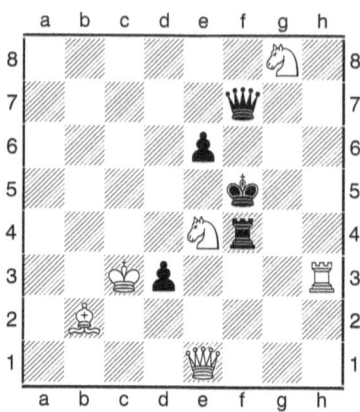

White to Play and Mate in 3

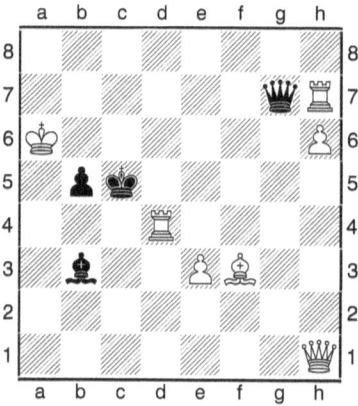

White to Play and Mate in 2

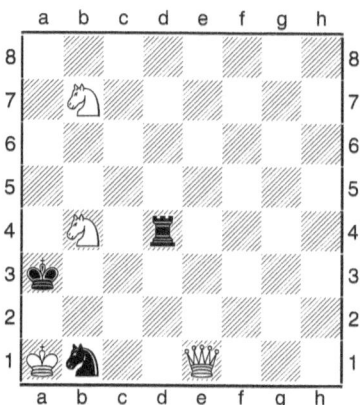

White to Play and Mate in 3

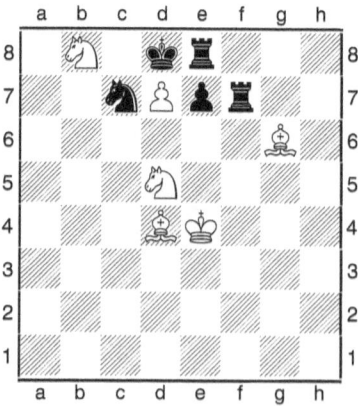

White to Play and Mate in 3

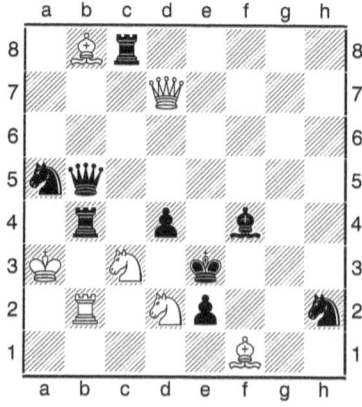

White to Play and Mate in 4

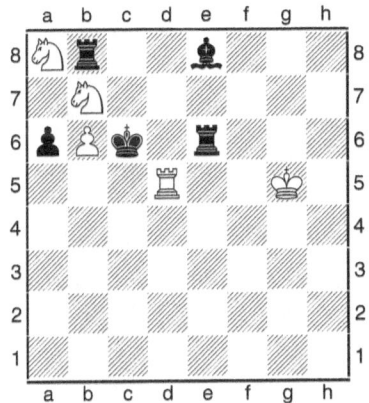

White to Play and Mate in 3

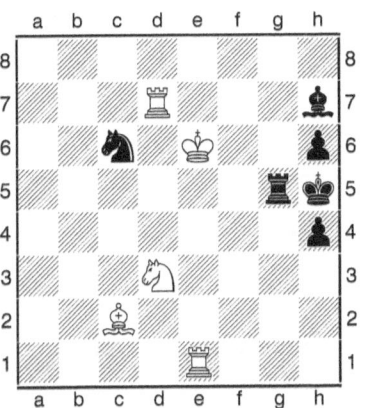

White to Play and Mate in 5

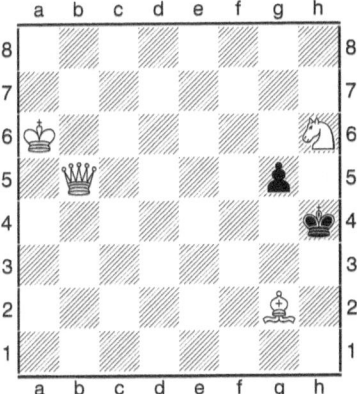

White to Play and Mate in 3

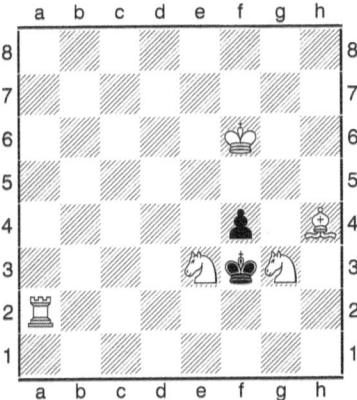

White to Play and Mate in 4

Now we begin with the BRS or 'baseline rejected' samples. The first sample of 20 compositions below is from BRS A. The NUS was compared against this (and also BRS B and BRS C) to test if there would be a difference between how the compositions in the NUS were being evaluated by the machine learning method compared to these known, rejected ones. All the BRS compositions were randomly selected.

BRS A

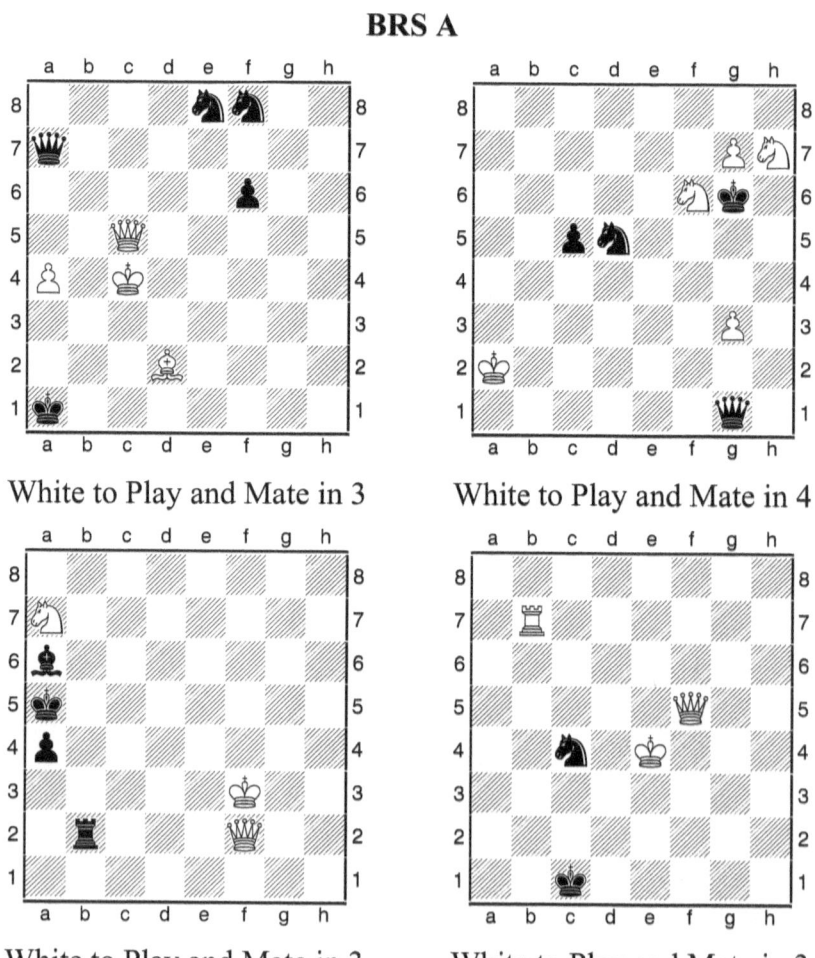

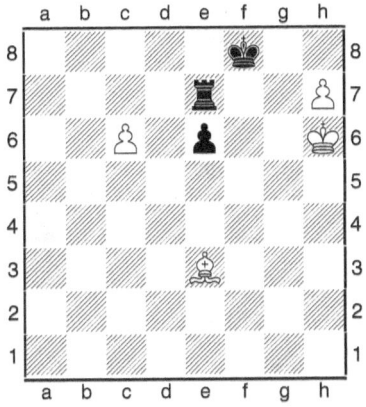

White to Play and Mate in 3

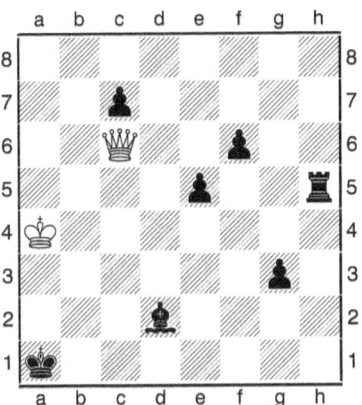

White to Play and Mate in 4

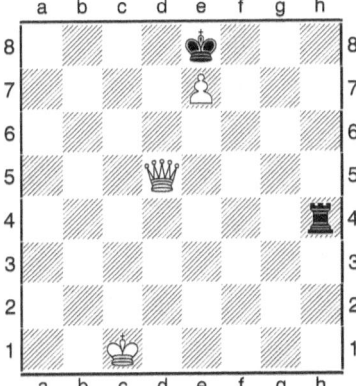

White to Play and Mate in 4

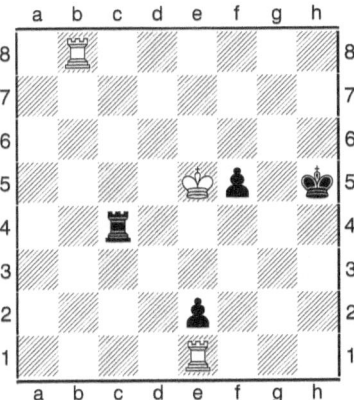

White to Play and Mate in 5

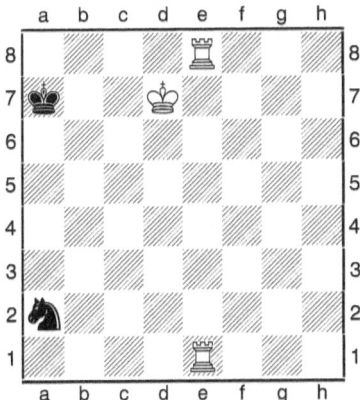

White to Play and Mate in 4

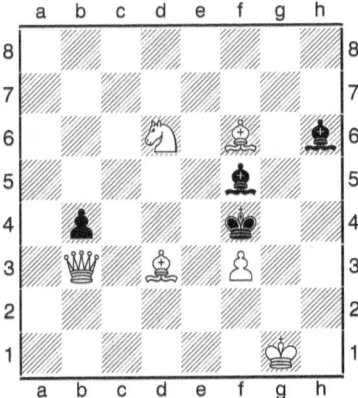

White to Play and Mate in 3

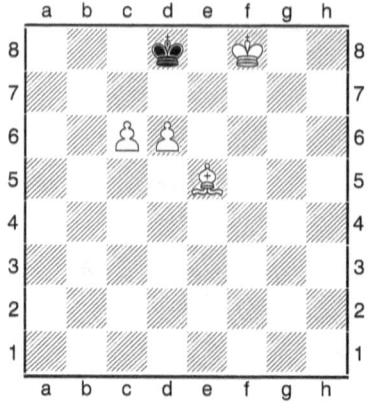

White to Play and Mate in 4

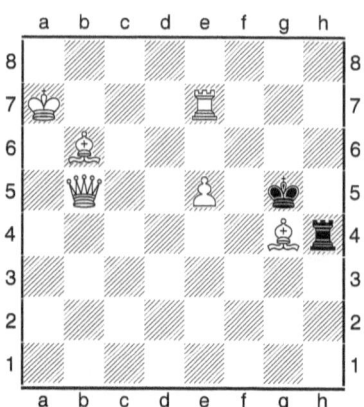

White to Play and Mate in 4

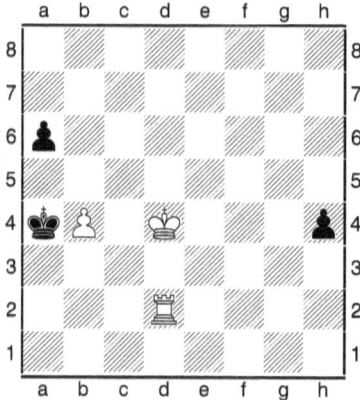

White to Play and Mate in 5

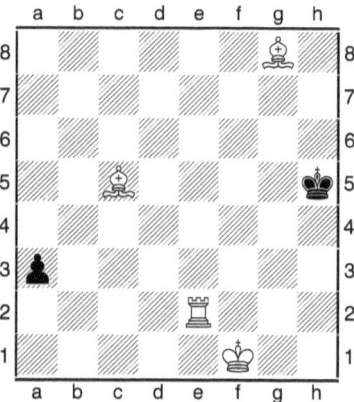

White to Play and Mate in 4

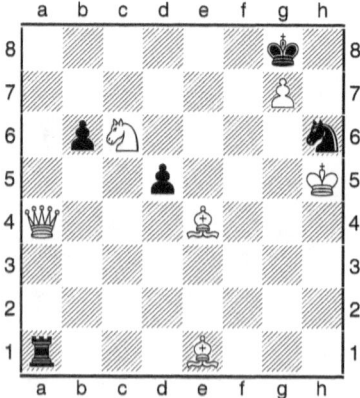

White to Play and Mate in 2

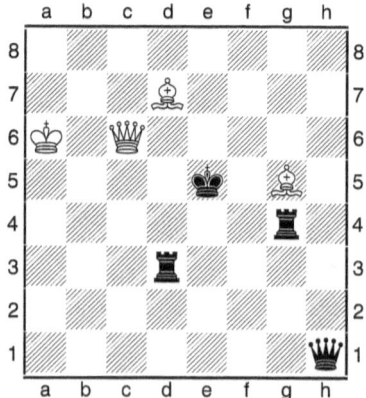

White to Play and Mate in 4

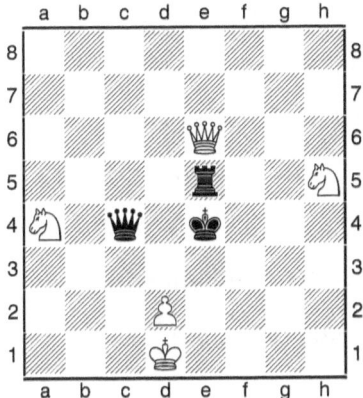
White to Play and Mate in 3

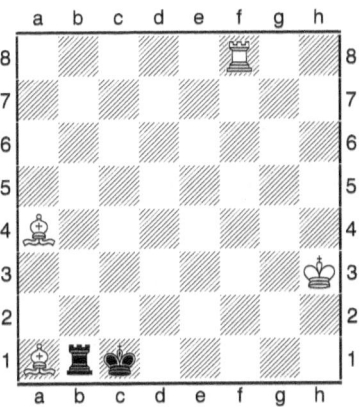
White to Play and Mate in 3

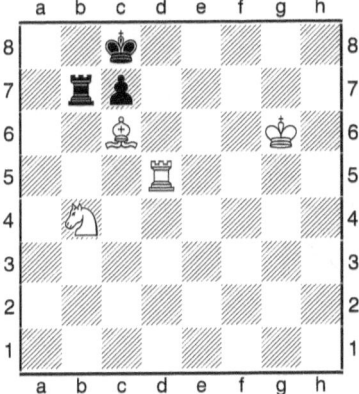
White to Play and Mate in 4

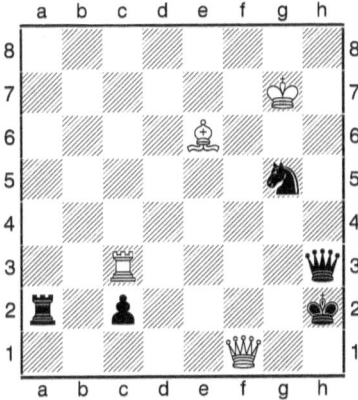
White to Play and Mate in 4

This is the second sample of 20 compositions or BRS B. The NUS was also compared against this sample and like with BRS A, differences were found which suggest that the machine learning method proposed is able to correctly learn user preferences. It is not clear yet how, exactly, it does this. Unlike an artificial neural network (ANN), there are no 'weights' that are being adjusted and it is also not yet clear if more data actually helps.

BRS B

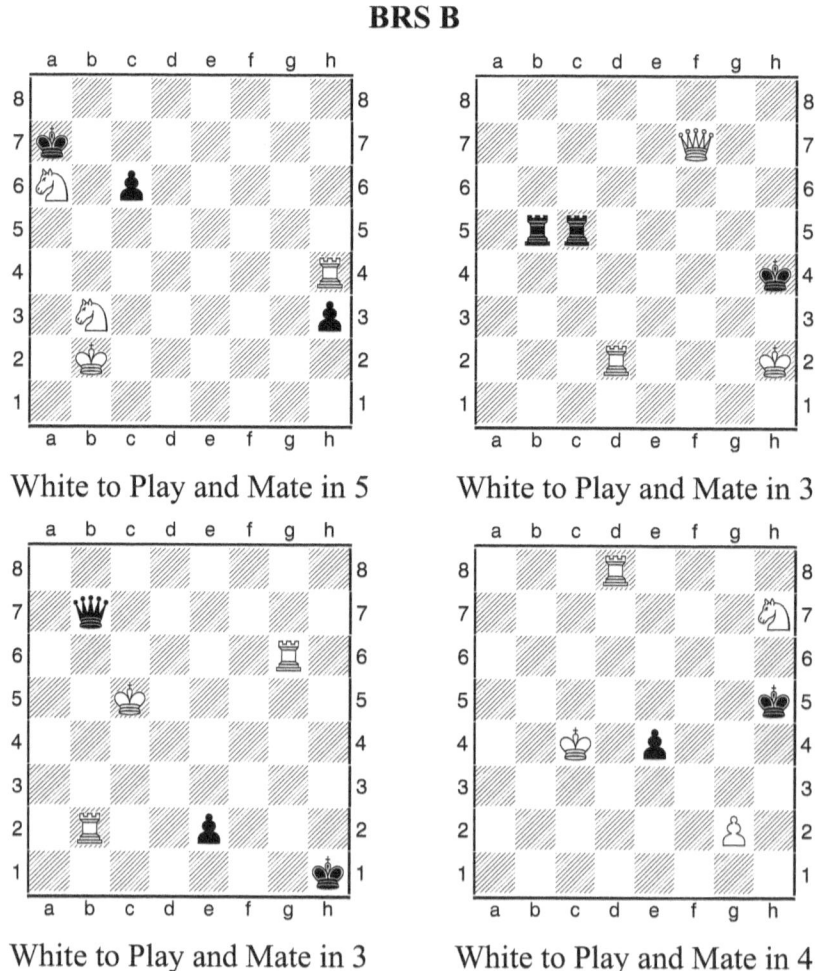

White to Play and Mate in 5

White to Play and Mate in 3

White to Play and Mate in 3

White to Play and Mate in 4

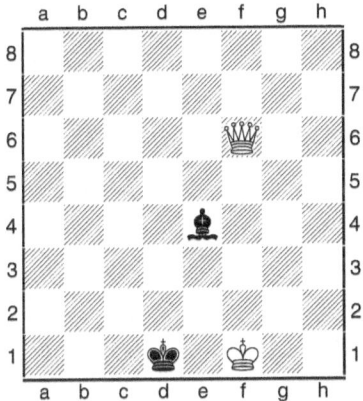

White to Play and Mate in 4

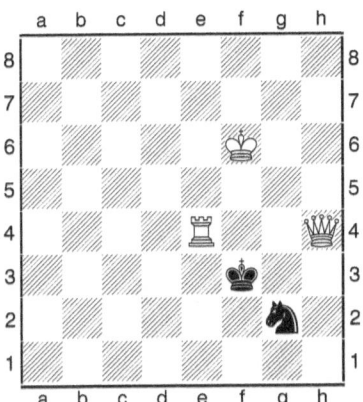

White to Play and Mate in 3

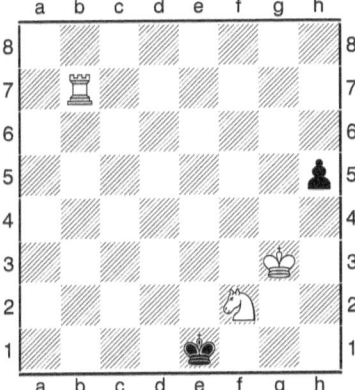

White to Play and Mate in 4

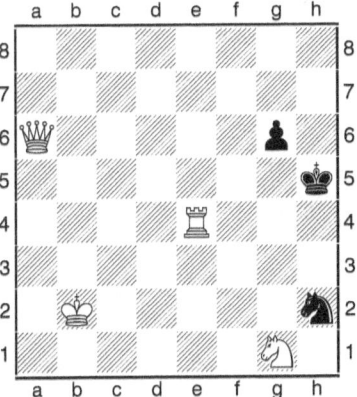

White to Play and Mate in 3

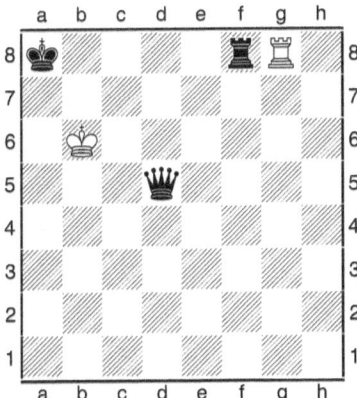

White to Play and Mate in 2

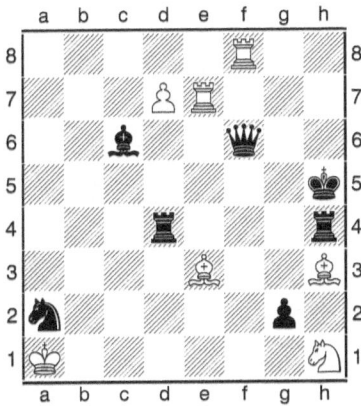

White to Play and Mate in 4

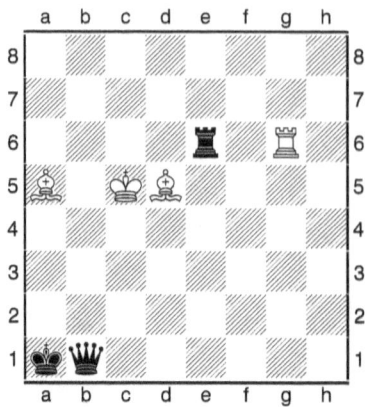

White to Play and Mate in 3

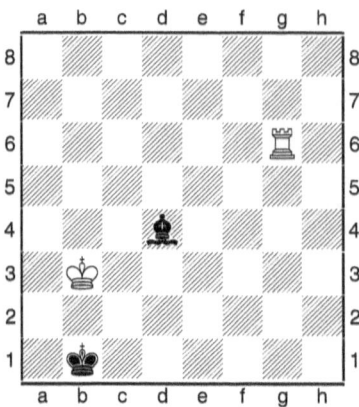

White to Play and Mate in 4

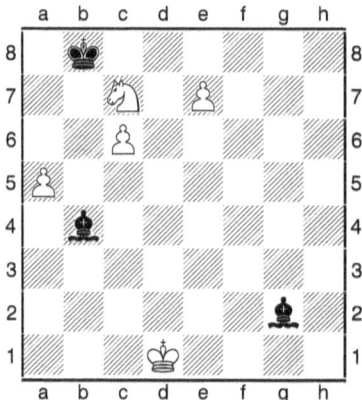

White to Play and Mate in 3

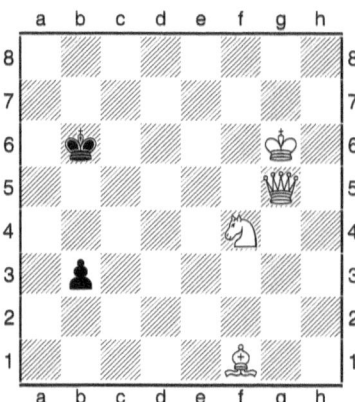

White to Play and Mate in 4

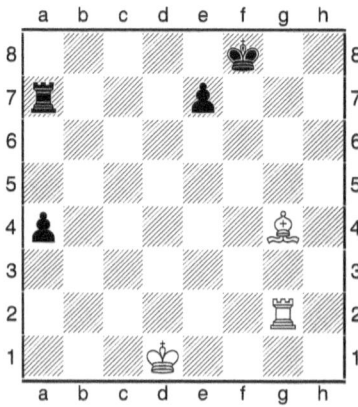

White to Play and Mate in 4

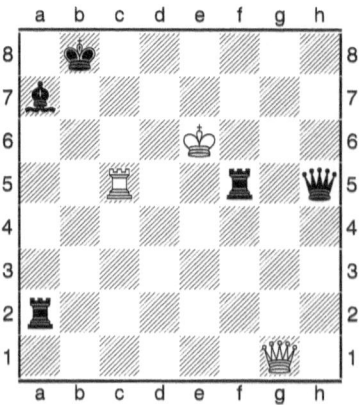

White to Play and Mate in 4

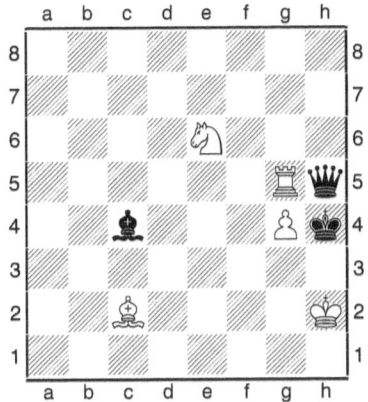

White to Play and Mate in 3

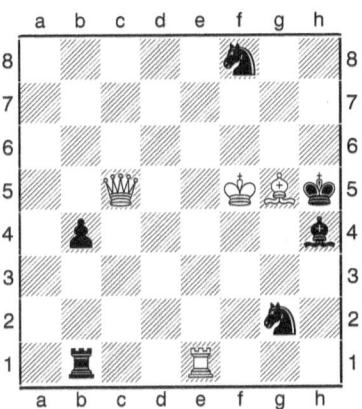

White to Play and Mate in 4

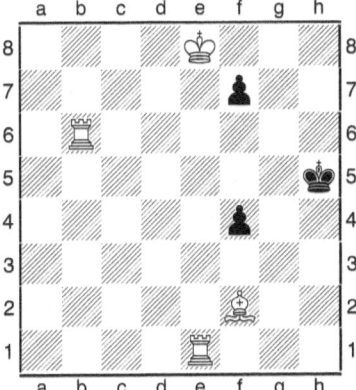

White to Play and Mate in 4

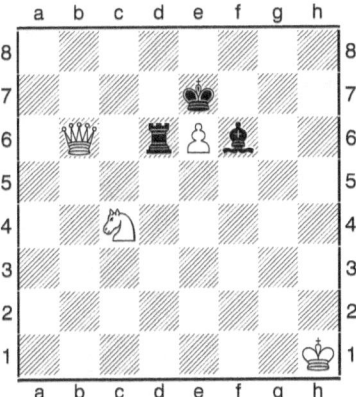

White to Play and Mate in 3

The third sample of 20 compositions or BRS C is presented below. The NUS was compared finally against this sample and like with BRS A and BRS B, differences were found which support the idea that the novel machine learning method is able to discern correctly between different collections. The consistency of the result against all three of these random samples is not something one would expect if there was no learning going on.

BRS C

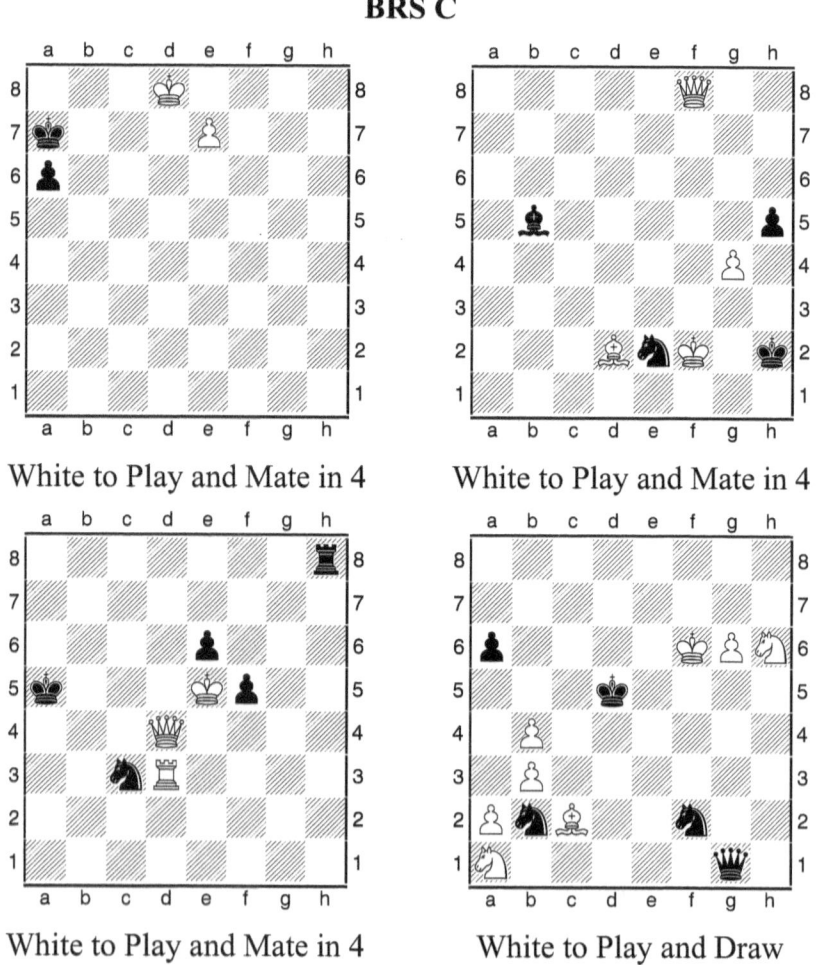

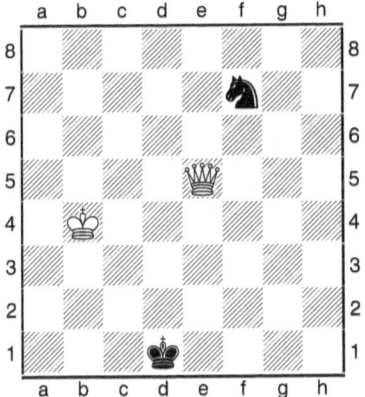

White to Play and Mate in 4

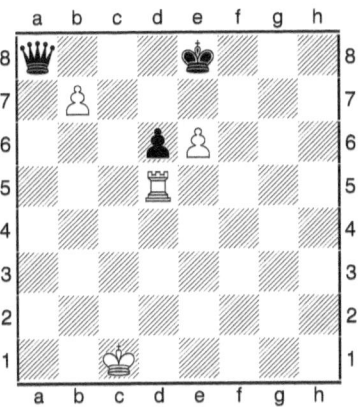

White to Play and Mate in 3

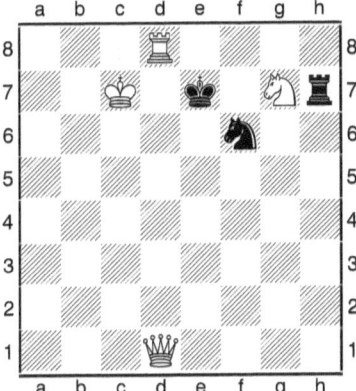

White to Play and Mate in 3

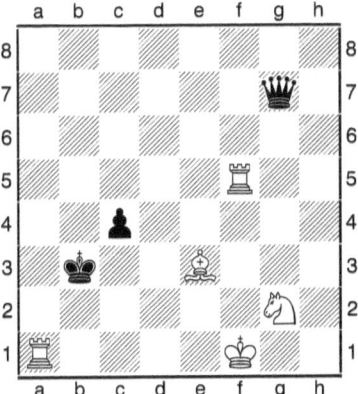

White to Play and Mate in 4

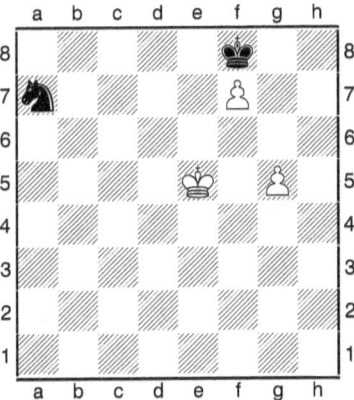

White to Play and Mate in 3

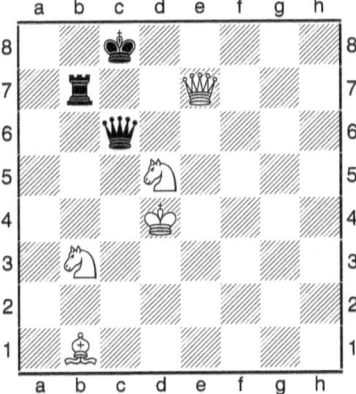

White to Play and Mate in 4

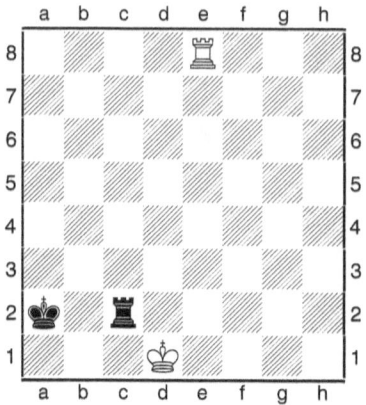

White to Play and Mate in 3

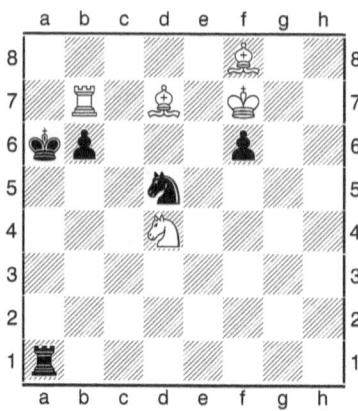

White to Play and Mate in 4

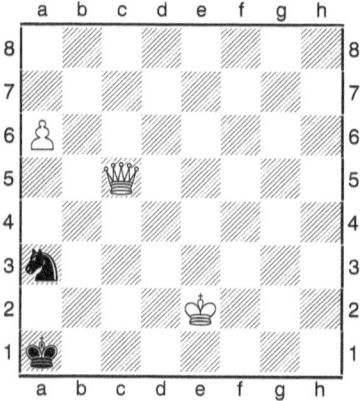

White to Play and Mate in 4

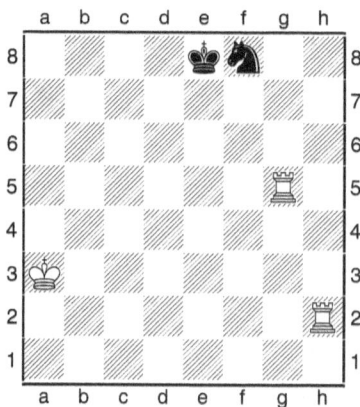

White to Play and Mate in 5

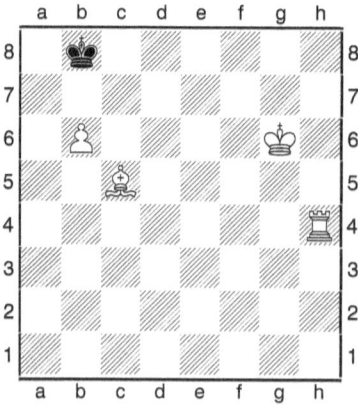

White to Play and Mate in 4

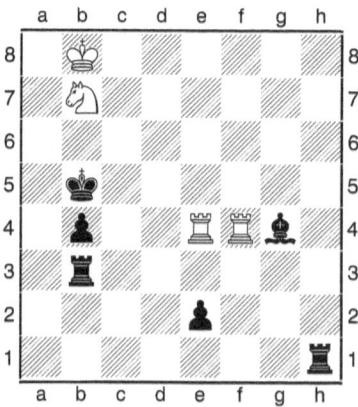

White to Play and Mate in 4

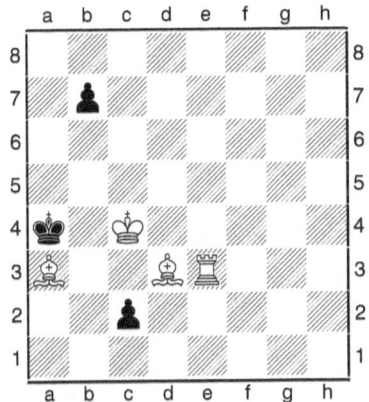

White to Play and Mate in 5

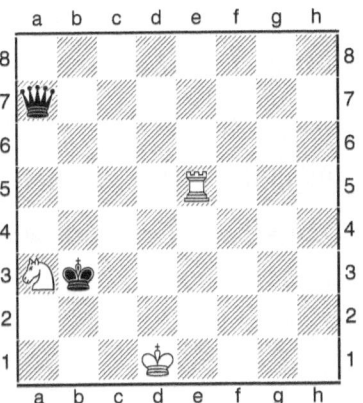

White to Play and Draw

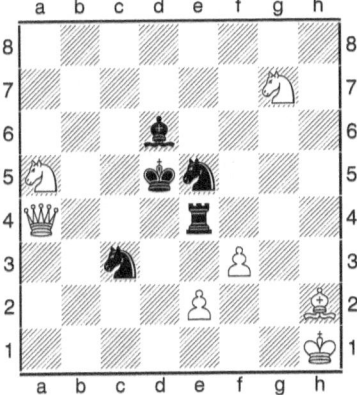

White to Play and Mate in 3

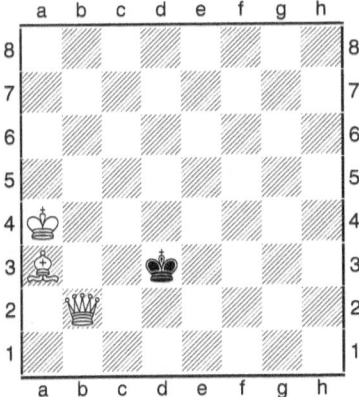

White to Play and Mate in 5

Now we move on to the second set of 'baseline rejected' samples or BRS2. The first of these is BRS2 A. NUS2, this time, was compared against this sample with the aim of confirming the results in the first experiment. If the machine learning method was valid, it should also work with a second 'new and unseen' sample compared against new baselines with comparable results, which it did (refer chapter 5 for more details).

BRS2 A

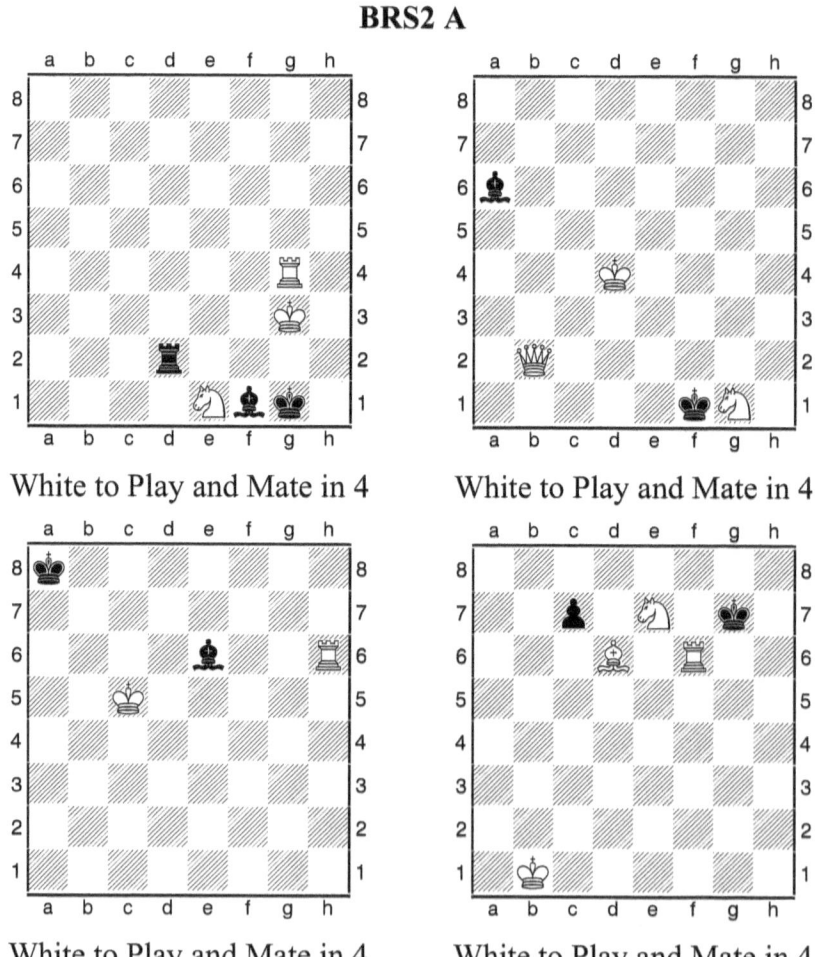

White to Play and Mate in 4

White to Play and Mate in 4

White to Play and Mate in 4

White to Play and Mate in 4

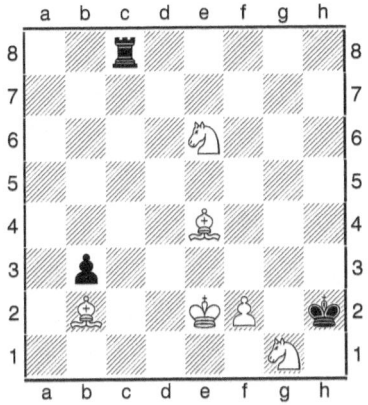

White to Play and Mate in 4

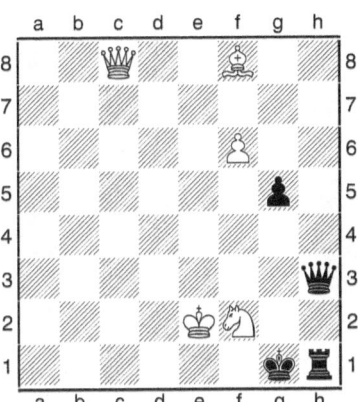

White to Play and Mate in 3

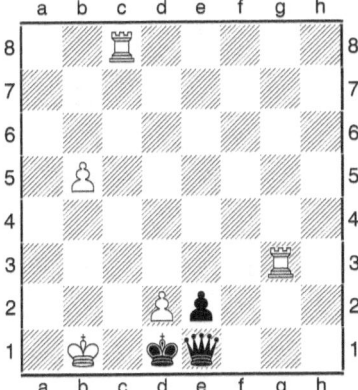

White to Play and Mate in 2

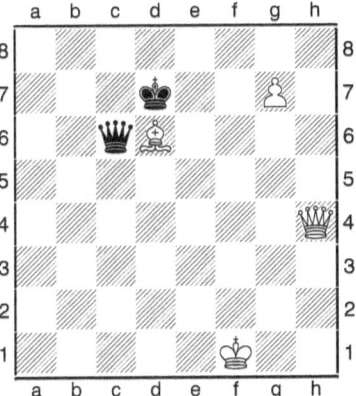

White to Play and Mate in 3

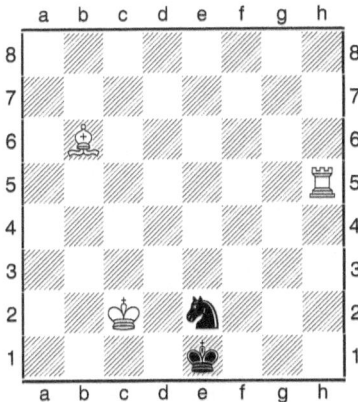

White to Play and Mate in 3

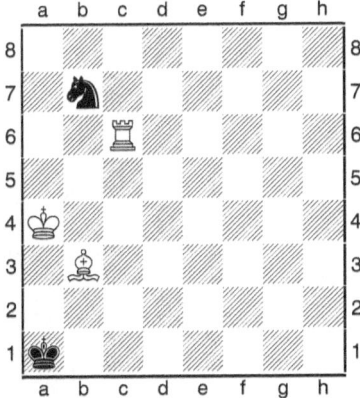

White to Play and Mate in 4

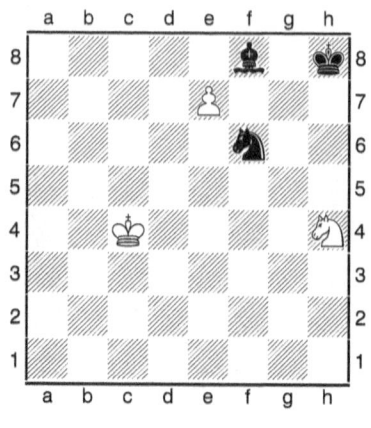

White to Play and Mate in 3

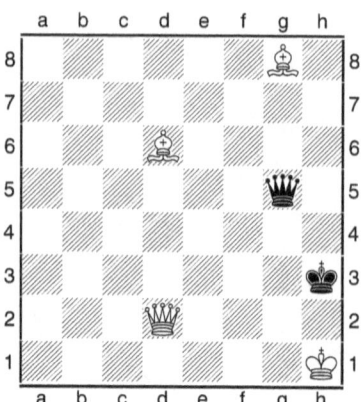

White to Play and Mate in 3

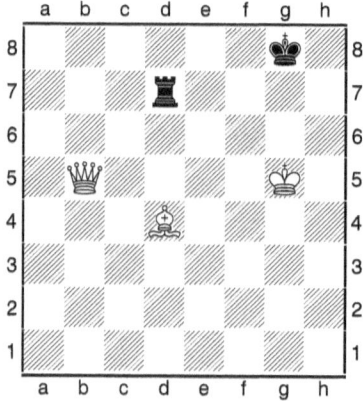

White to Play and Mate in 3

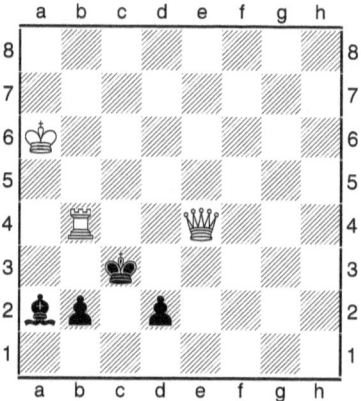

White to Play and Mate in 3

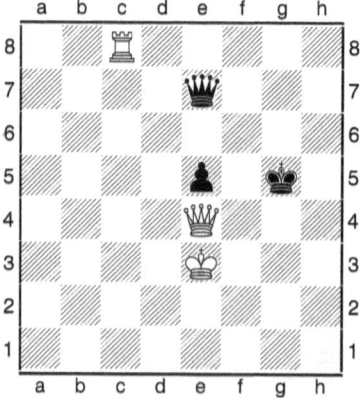

White to Play and Mate in 3

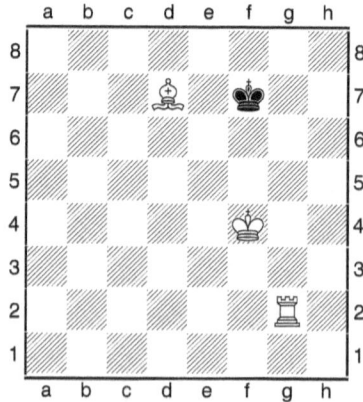

White to Play and Mate in 5

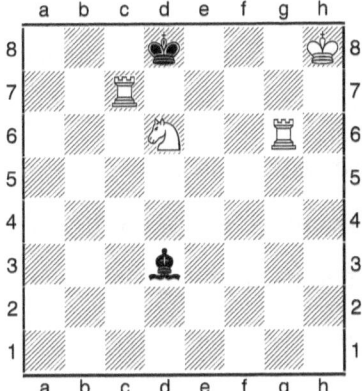
White to Play and Mate in 3

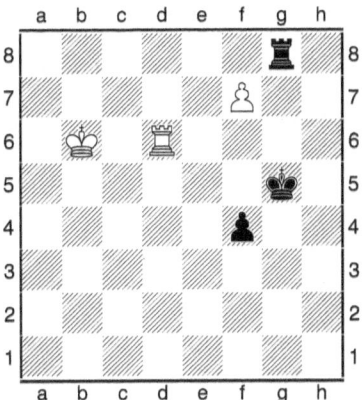
White to Play and Mate in 3

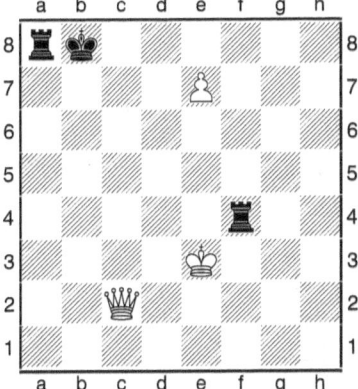
White to Play and Mate in 3

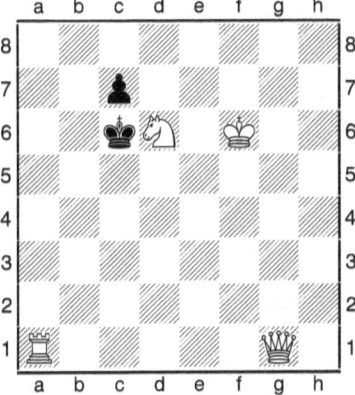
White to Play and Mate in 3

The next 'baseline rejected' sample was BRS2 B. The NUS2 was also compared against it and the results were still consistent with the previous sample and the first experiment. It is not yet known if the machine learning method would be as consistent, perhaps even better, if the 'liked' and 'disliked' collections used were limited to just one type of problem, e.g. mates in 3, in order to make predictions from 'new and unseen' mates of the same type.

BRS2 B

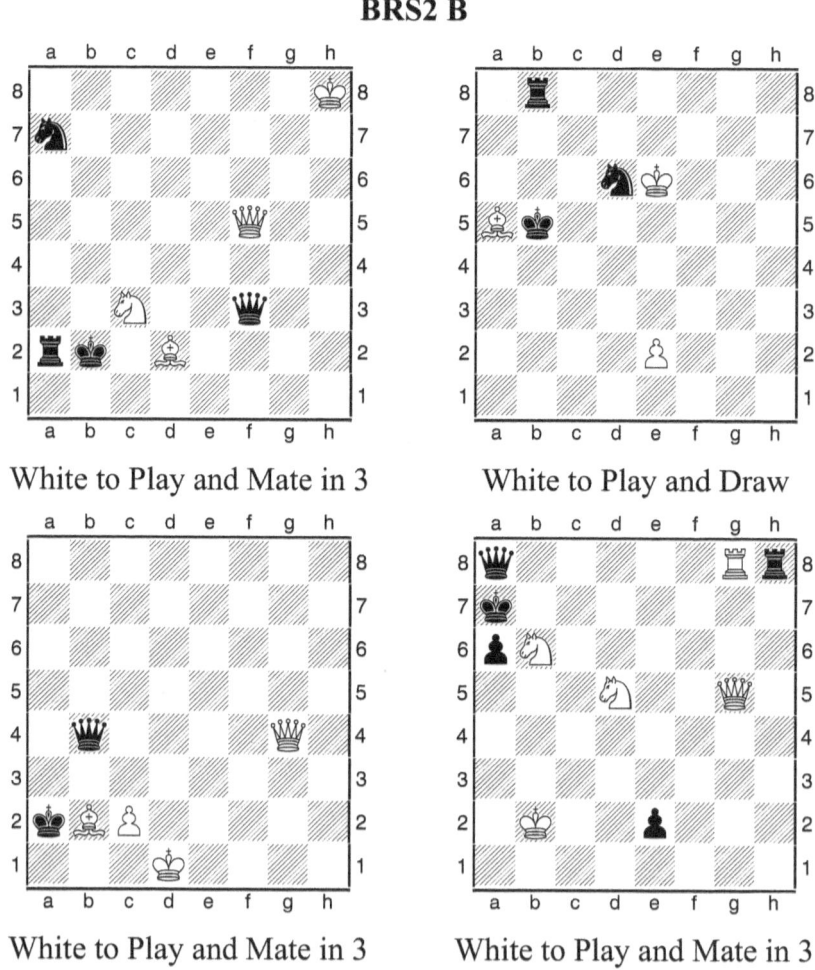

White to Play and Mate in 3

White to Play and Draw

White to Play and Mate in 3

White to Play and Mate in 3

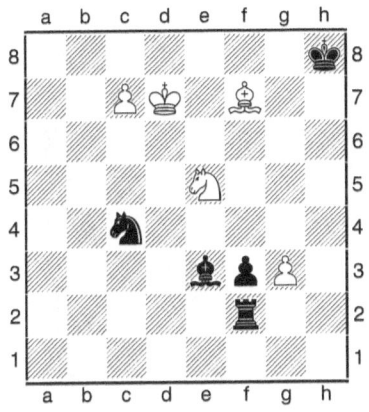

White to Play and Mate in 4

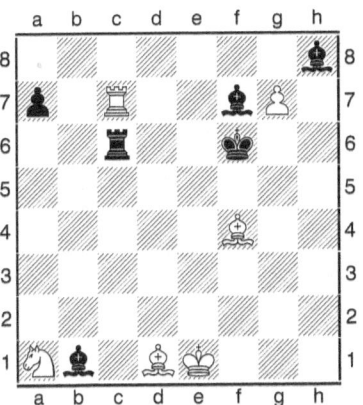

White to Play and Mate in 5

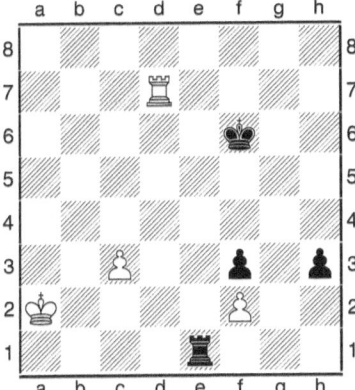

White to Play and Draw

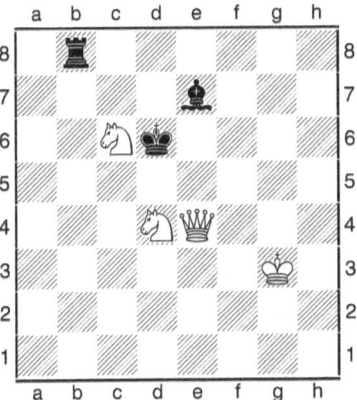

White to Play and Mate in 3

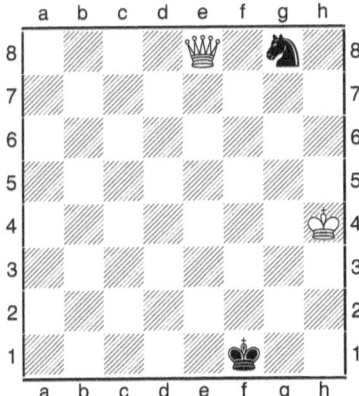

White to Play and Mate in 4

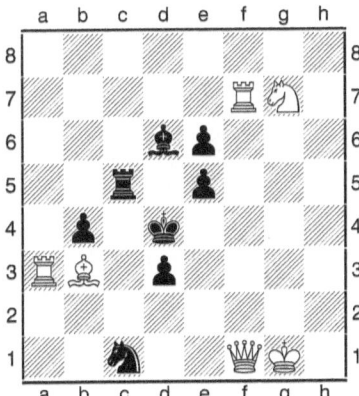

White to Play and Mate in 3

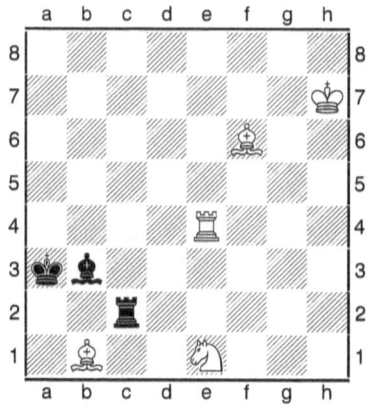

White to Play and Mate in 3

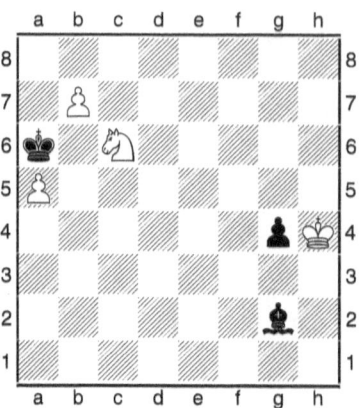

White to Play and Mate in 2

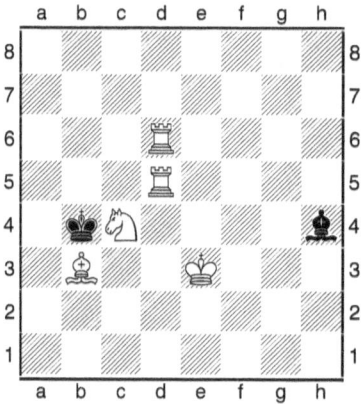

White to Play and Mate in 2

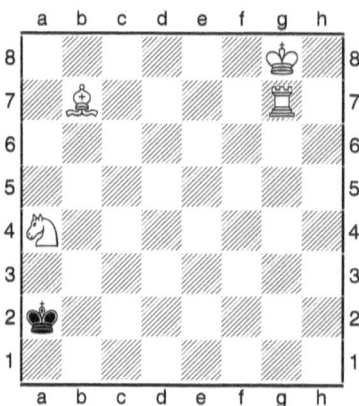

White to Play and Mate in 5

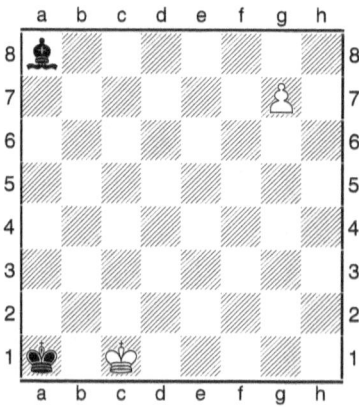

White to Play and Mate in 3

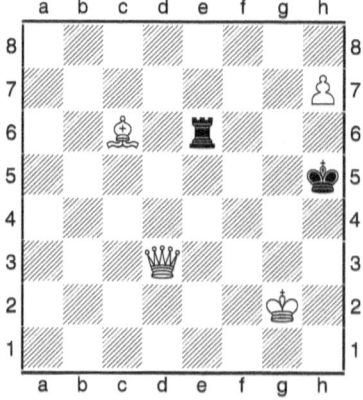

White to Play and Mate in 3

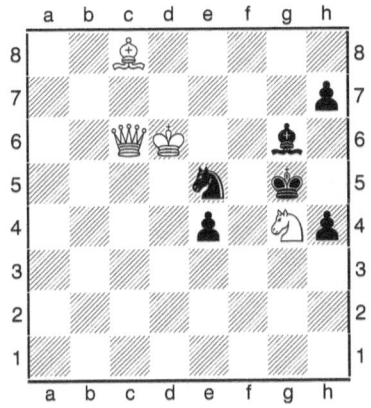

White to Play and Mate in 3

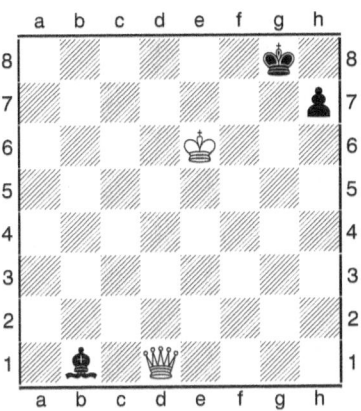

White to Play and Mate in 3

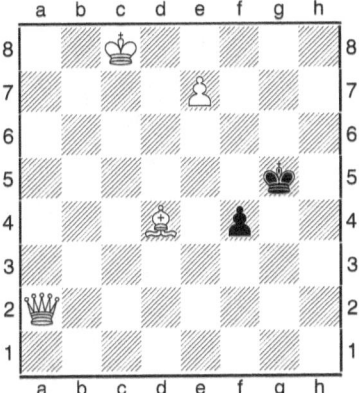

White to Play and Mate in 3

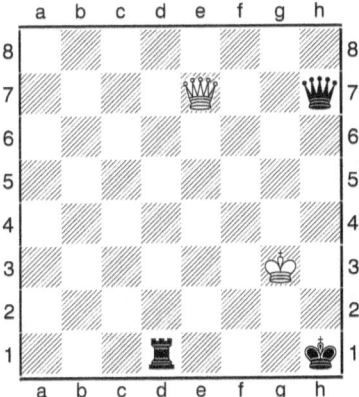

White to Play and Mate in 3

The final sample, BRS2 C, is shown below. Overall, the results were consistent, if not better, than the first experiment. There are still many open questions with regard to the proposed machine learning method. In particular, relating to the ideal size of samples, randomization (or not) and the number of cycles used. Also in balancing between the right amount of materials to learn from for the best results (considering speed as well).

BRS2 C

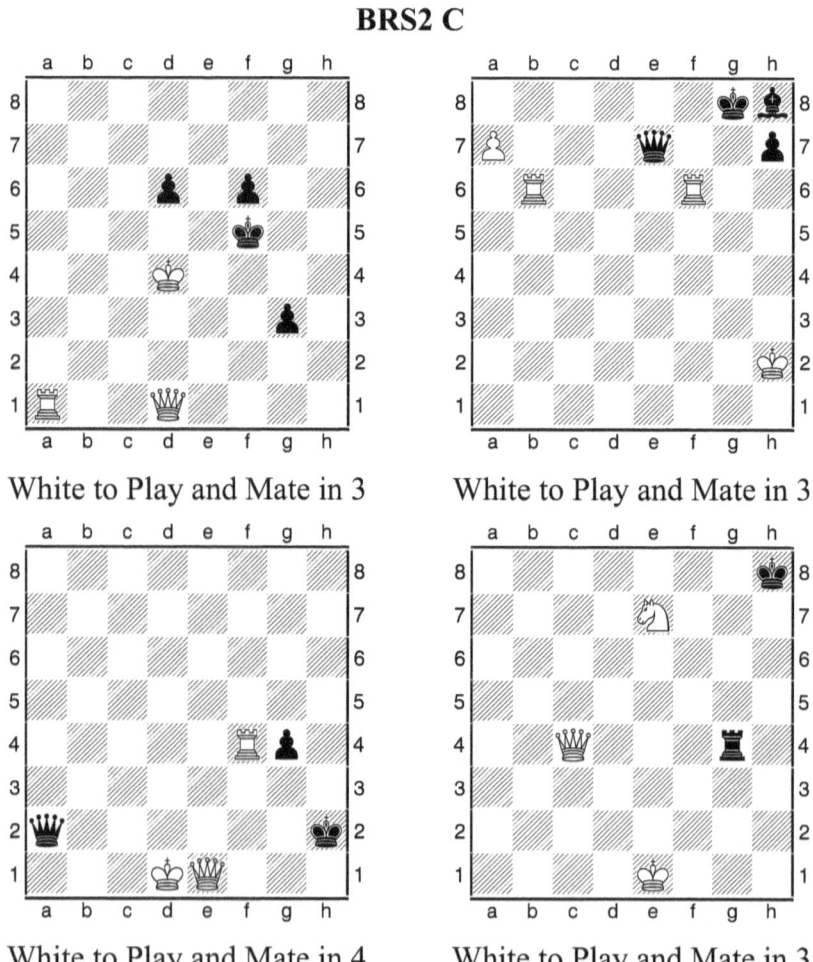

White to Play and Mate in 3

White to Play and Mate in 3

White to Play and Mate in 4

White to Play and Mate in 3

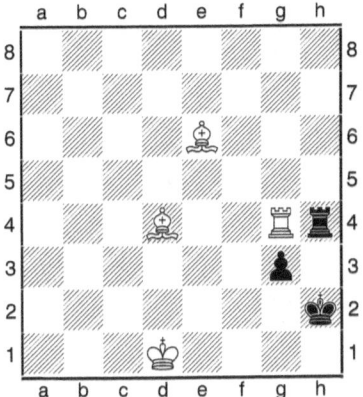

White to Play and Mate in 3

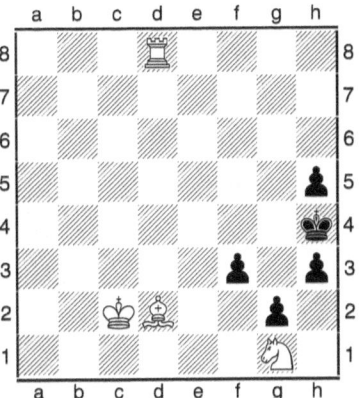

White to Play and Mate in 3

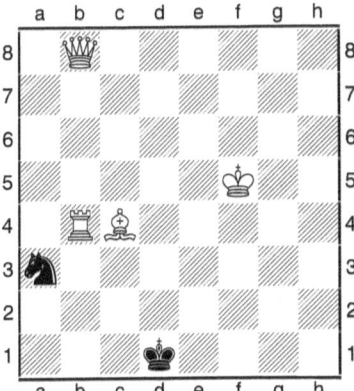

White to Play and Mate in 3

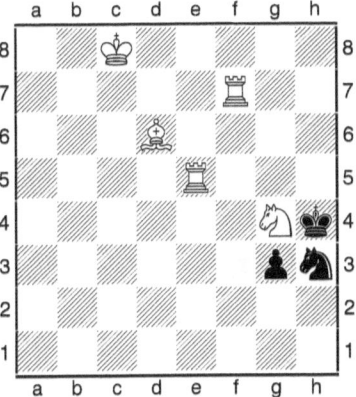

White to Play and Mate in 3

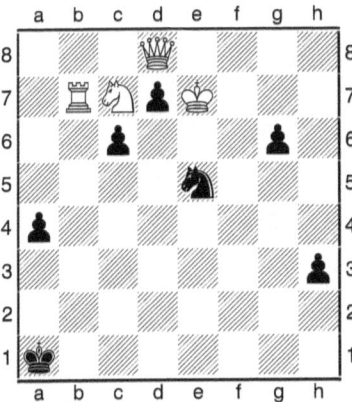

White to Play and Mate in 3

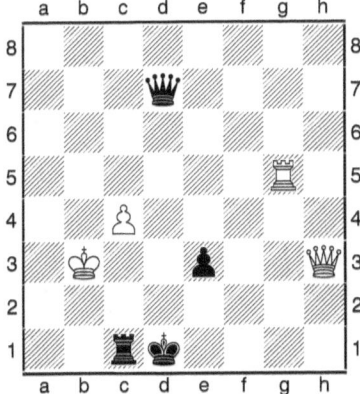

White to Play and Mate in 3

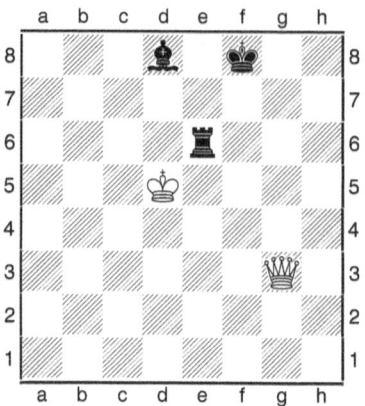

White to Play and Mate in 3

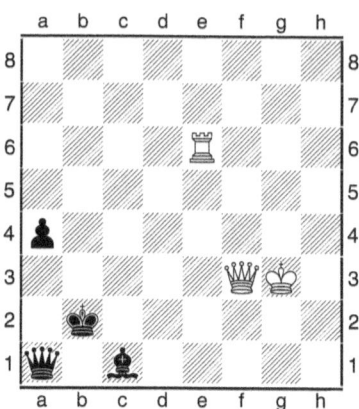

White to Play and Mate in 3

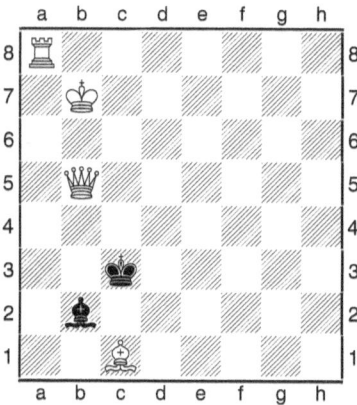

White to Play and Mate in 3

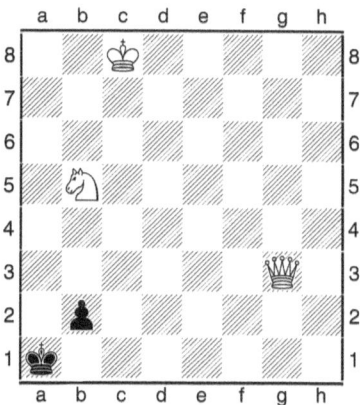

White to Play and Mate in 4

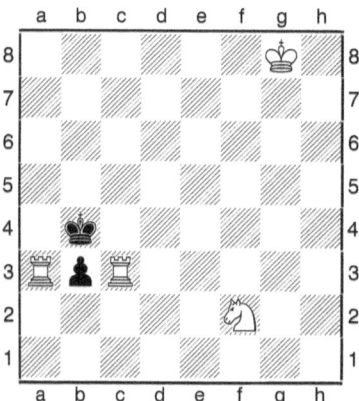

White to Play and Mate in 3

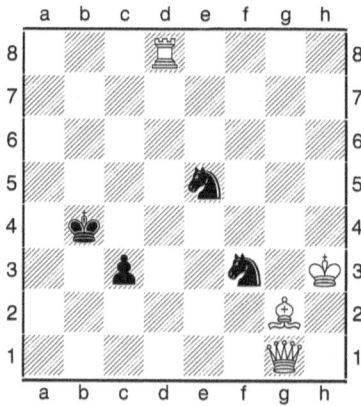

White to Play and Mate in 3

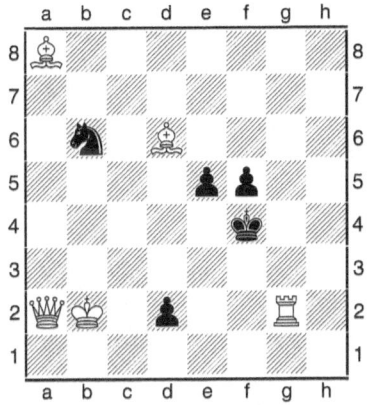
White to Play and Mate in 4

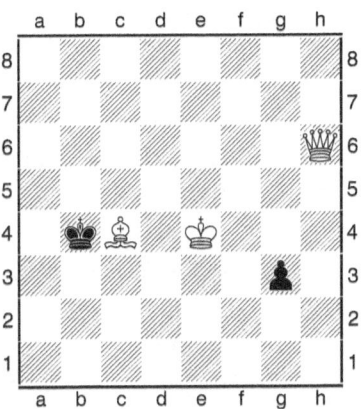
White to Play and Mate in 4

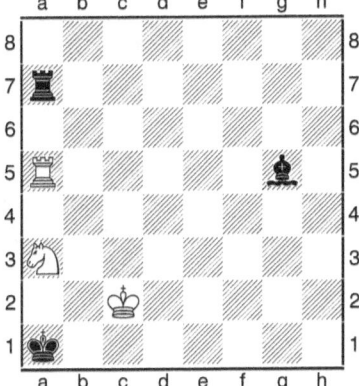
White to Play and Mate in 4

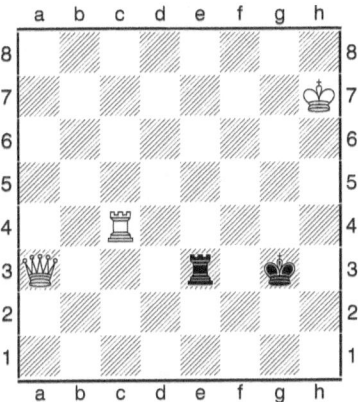
White to Play and Mate in 3

Previous Books by Azlan Iqbal

1. *Chesthetica's Book of Chess Constructs, Volume 4: Original Computer-Generated Chess Problems for Solving and Analysis*, Kindle Direct Publishing, Washington, United States, 2020, eISBN 978-983-808-249-5.

2. *Chesthetica's Book of Chess Constructs, Volume 3: Original Computer-Generated Chess Problems for Solving and Analysis*, Kindle Direct Publishing, Washington, United States, 2019, eISBN 978-983-808-248-8.

3. *Chesthetica's Book of Chess Constructs, Volume 2: Original Computer-Generated Chess Problems for Solving and Analysis*, Kindle Direct Publishing, Washington, United States, 2018, eISBN 978-983-808-246-4.

4. *Chesthetica's Book of Chess Constructs, Volume 1: Original Computer-Generated Chess Problems for Solving and Analysis*, Kindle Direct Publishing, Washington, United States, 2017, eISBN 978-983-808-244-0.

5. *The Digital Synaptic Neural Substrate: A New Approach to Computational Creativity*, 1st Edition, SpringerBriefs in Cognitive Computation, Springer International Publishing, Switzerland, 2016, eISBN 978-3-319-28079-0.

www.ingramcontent.com/pod-product-compliance
Lightning Source LLC
Chambersburg PA
CBHW031432210526
45464CB00005B/2157